What **experts** are saying abo[ut]
The Tao of Tai Chi: The Ma[king of a New Science]

"I just finished this book, and I can[not help but be struck]
with synchronicity--and a book like [this. The Tai]
Chi world has needed a book like this for a long time!"
-- Dr. Pete Gryffin, University of Florida Alumni Fellow, author of "Tai Chi Therapy: The Science of Metarobics," founder of the Metarobic Institute

"Bill Douglas, founder of World Tai Chi Day, has written a revealing, heartfelt book about his personal journey and its universal implications. Delving into the worlds of science, spirituality and martial arts, it's the fascinating story of a small town boy who discovers his path, finds his mission and succeeds in spreading the amazing practices of Tai Chi and Qigong around the world. There are many valuable lessons to be learned from this illuminating book."
**-- Barry Strugatz, director of the documentary,
THE PROFESSOR: TAI CHI'S JOURNEY WEST**

"*The Tao of Tai Chi* was the answer to my longing to learn more about Tao. From the beginning till the end I was fascinated ..."
-- Hilda Cardinaels, Tai Chi Teacher, Belgium

"This is an addition any serious student of Tai Chi should add to their collection! Tai Chi is much larger than the martial applications, Bill's book tackles more than the nuts and bolts and deals with what makes it work! This is a book you can read again and again, one you can contemplate with!"
**-- Dave Pickens, National Co-Chairman of Kung Fu AAU, previous National Chairman Chinese Martial Arts Division
United States Amateur Athletic Union**

"This book can shift the "earth below and the heaven above", not just your Tai Chi and Qigong journey, but the way you see and live your life in the universe. *The Tao of Tai Chi: The Making of a New Science* may become a tectonic shifting point for the Tai Chi and Qigong world to become a major force for all in the realization of love and compassion in our world. It can make an imperative and essential positive impact on our ailing health and life systems.
 Bill's deep understanding of "The Qi" lends him to combine spirit and science in a real livable productive path. This is a '**must read**' for everyone. The contents could even be a foundation for an educational movie!"
-- Dame Dr. Effie Chow PhD, RN, LiAc(CA), DiplAc(NCCAOM), Qigong Grandmaster, Founder and President, East West Academy of Healing Arts and Chow Medical Qigong, Founder of the annual World Congress on Qigong/Tai Chi/Traditional Chinese Medicine in its' 17th year, Appointee to President Bill Clinton's White House Commission on

Complementary and Alternative Medicine Policy. Faculty of the University of Hawaii, John A. Burn Medical School Division of Integrative Medicine CAM

"*The Tao of Tai Chi* is a magical book ... Each page, each paragraph, each picture tell us that Qigong and Tai Chi, more than just a psychophysical exercise, is really a profound art, science, study and poetry ... It reveals how the movements we perform in Internal Arts, uniting our body and our breathing, can open us to *infinite miracles!*"
-- Professor Jose Milton de Olivera, Honorary Advisor of Square of the Universal Harmony, Being Tao Association, Brasilia, Brazil

"After reading *The Tao of Tai Chi: The Making of a New Science* I feel like I have been credited with 100 more years and wisdom. This is a book I will meditate on over and over again! Some books are made to be read by lips and others with the heart. This book is a real testimony of a man who isn't only an expert of the subject, but also an authentic seeker whose personal experience is highly relevant to all of us. The extraordinary level of information, personal experiences and anecdotes he makes available to us, has resulted in a wonderful book which will obviously impact the world. The generosity of heart and the knowledge Bill shows will give you this strange feeling of being at home while moving from chapter to chapter."
-- Master Ariel Betti, Founder of FITAQI/ Active Promoter of Tai Chi/ Qigong and Meditation in Africa

"I LOVED THIS BOOK, really lovely! This book took me into a very deep trip internally and what I liked the most was that Bill was able to connect Art with philosophy, science, and more specifically with consciousness science in a way that seemed so very easy and simple, as simply elegant as a flower opening. It is an awakening tool for everyone to realize how strong is our inner and how it feels easy and simple when we are connected to our true self. It highlights how important that balancing the self and reaching harmony is the way of well being and a better life."
-- Mohamed Essa, Chromatic Healing Founder, Cairo, Egyptian Official World Tai Chi & Qigong Day, World Healing Day Organizer, Cairo, Egypt

"This latest book from World Tai Chi Day founder Bill Douglas is a must read for all tai chi practitioners from beginners to grand masters. I consider Bill to be a visionary and his tireless efforts to get the " Tai Chi word" out there is so inspiring . I hope this book makes it into the bestsellers list as it is such a deserving publication. Keep up the amazing work that you do Bill. "
-- Bev Abela, Tai Chi @ The Beach, Perth, Australia

Read complete expert's comments in back of book ...

About the Author:

Bill Douglas, Founder of World Tai Chi & Qigong Day, was "2009's Inductee to the World Internal Arts Hall of Fame" in New York; Recipient of the National Qigong Association's "Extraordinary Service in the Field of Qigong Award"; Recipient of the World Congress on Qigong in San Francisco's "Qigong Media Excellence Award"; Author of a best-selling Tai Chi book sold worldwide in several languages, "The Complete Idiot's Guide to T'ai Chi & Qigong" (4th edition, Bantam-Penguin, New York).

Bill has been a Tai Chi source for: *The New York Times; Wall Street Journal;* BBC World Radio; *South China Morning Post;* China's Xinhua News Agency; and media worldwide. He was commissioned to create a Tai Chi tutorial for *Prevention Magazine's* article on 'boosting your immune system with Tai Chi.' He has taught Tai Chi Meditation for many of the world's largest corporations, public/special education, drug/prison rehabilitation programs, and for many of the world's largest health networks, including several current ongoing programs for the University of Kansas Hospital's Turning Point Center for Hope and Healing. A DVD he created has been provided to patients by physicians and neurologists all across America. His classes and teaching have profoundly changed people's lives, according to a virtually endless list of his student/reader/DVD viewer comments and reviews from around the world.

Bill Douglas has dedicated much of his life to helping other Tai Chi and Qigong teachers and mind body teachers around the world to expand their teaching and publicize their local classes, via his public service work organizing World Tai Chi & Qigong Day each year for nearly 2 decades. All the 100s of pages of resources at WorldTaiChiDay.org (official website of this event) are a free public service designed to connect the public with all teachers worldwide who are invited to list their schools for free. This event was created by Bill to foster the evolution of a healthier, calmer, and more peaceful world.

"Your organizing of this global event has been very helpful in gaining media attention for the benefits of Qi Gong & Tai Chi and in creating awareness of our school and classes. New people come to our World Tai Chi & Qi Gong Day event every year."
-- Howard Fraracci, Qi Gong teacher, **Toronto, Canada**

"Our Tai Chi programs continue to grow and our numbers of Tai Chi Schools continue to grow at a phenomenal rate and I feel your efforts are fueling this growth worldwide and we are all in awe of what the World Tai Chi & Qigong Day has done."
-- Dave Pickens, **National Chairman Chinese Martial Arts Division United States Amateur Athletic Union**

"World Tai Chi & Qigong Day is the most significant contribution to promoting the art of T'ai Chi and Qigong today ... thanks to you; the possibilities are unlimited."
-- Ken Ryan, Sifu at Maine Coast Taijiquan, **Maine USA**

"Words cannot express feelings, only acts do. I'm sure when you created the World Tai Chi & Qigong Day, you did not imagine that it would be celebrated all over the world and grow so fast. You drove all of us in the path of One World... One Breath. Step by step, we would reach to One Mind... One Spirit. Thank you."
-- Professor Jose Milton de Olivera - Being Tao Association / Square of Universal Harmony. **Brasília, Brazil**

"A reflection of how successful the invasion has been is World Tai Chi Day, organized by Bill Douglas. One of the purposes of this day is 'to bring together people across racial, economic, religious, and geo-political boundaries, to join together for the purpose of health and healing, providing an example to the world." Millions of people around the world – 65 nations participated in 2011 – gather one day each year to celebrate the health and healing benefits of Tai Chi and Qigong."
-- *The Harvard Medical School Guide to Tai Chi, page 25*

Sifu Mohamed Essa leads World Tai Chi & Qigong Day 2016 celebration attendees in Cairo, Egypt in Tiger Qigong … joining 80 other nations events.

* Cairo's WTCQD celebrations have been supported by the Chinese and Indian government's Egyptian embassies, and by the Egyptian Ministry of Tourism.

"One World … One Breath" WTCQD's event motto.

Dedication …

To my mother-in-law, Sheung Oi Wong, a Tai Chi player, a woman who endured more than I can imagine and yet emerged on the other side with grace, dignity, and a quiet power that left me in awe of the human spirit.

To my mother, Evelyn Douglas, a woman who walked through a life of hardness that would break most people, and yet emerged as a siren of love and compassion so sweet she would break an angel's heart--the greatest minister God ever created, and I cannot believe I lived in her house and walked on this planet with one such as her.

To my wife, my partner, my fellow warrior in light, my angel, Angela Oi Yue Wong, who is the only reason I still exist on this planet. As you will see in this book, I am convinced that such a woman was chosen to be by my side from our earliest childhood, even though we were born and raised on opposite sides of the planet.

Lao Tzu extolled us to *know the masculine* Yang world, but to *keep to the feminine,* the Yin – the *mother* of all things.

Illumination Corporation Publishing and SMARTaichi Publishing

www.IlluminationCorporation.com

www.SMARTaichi.com

Copyright © 2016 by William Douglas

Published by CreateSpace for
Illumination Corporation Publishing and
SMARTaichi Publishing

ISBN-13:
978-1537117935

ISBN-10:
1537117939

All rights reserved. Published in the United States by CreateSpace for Illumination Corporation Publishing and SMARTaichi Publishing. No part of this publication may be reproduced in any way without the written permission of the author. Contact him at www.IlluminationCorporation.com or at www.SMARTaichi.com

Book design by Illumination Corporation and SMARTaichi Artistic Designs

For orders, you may search your distribution lists for the ISBN of this book, or contact Illumination Corporation publishing at
www.IlluminationCorporation.com,
www.SMARTaichi.com
or call 1-913-648-2256

First Edition

THE TAO OF PUSH HANDS ...

I recently got a call from a young person who heard I taught Push Hands in my classes, and said he was not interested in learning Moving Qigong, or Tai Chi, or Sitting Qigong, or Taoist philosophy. He only wanted to learn Push Hands. My mind traveled back to what it was that had led to my grasp of Push Hands today.

I remembered a long journey beginning so long ago; meeting a Taoist Monk in a Taoist Temple in Hong Kong, countless hours of going within during Moving Qigong and Tai Chi practices that I did not understand the reason for at the time.

I remembered the hours and hours of Standing Post observing the tangles in my mind and body and using the Qigong breathing and the Qi to untangle those knots in my mind, heart, and body, and mostly I remembered the *years of studying the Tao te Ching* which I did in order to try to make sense of experiences this internal Tai Chi and Qigong study was unfolding in me ... all of this is what eventually evolved into the way I Push Hands today. My Push Hands ability today is only the tiny visible tip of a deep wave, a vast ocean of events and experiences, all being the force beneath what one can now glimpse in my Push Hands.

You see, when I began Qigong I did not understand why I was moving my pelvis around in circles, or thinking of my spine elongating, or any of the other myriad things I was being taught to do. It wasn't like any exercise I had done before; I couldn't feel my muscles burning or anything. I saw no productivity in it. To stick with it, I just had to surrender to something larger than I could understand at that time. Same thing with my Sitting Qigong meditations, they seemed so strange and intangible, I never thought I was doing them right, my mind was wandering all the time. And even more so the Standing Qigong Meditation, Gathering Qi, or Standing Post, made no sense at all to me at first. I thought, 'Why am I standing here like this? My shoulders are tight, my back hurts! This is nuts! What a waste of time! I wasn't DOING anything!'

I spent hours and hours Standing Post, and then eventually all of this chaos began to *gel* into a bigger picture. The Nei Gong Sitting Qigong meditation revealed my energetic nature, and how the tension and pressure we feel is really energy knots in this field or energetic being we are. I began to understand that when I was Standing Post I wasn't supposed to just macho through it and bear the pain, it was a vehicle for me to see how and where I tend to hold the knots in my field, my mind, heart, and body – and then use the Qigong breathing and the image of Qi to allow those knots to begin to untangle.

I began to see how Standing Post, or rather the internal insights it shines light upon, translated into me learning how to loosen around my Tai Chi forms, and to surrender and sink into them, and they became more of a flow and less of an effort. They became more fun and less work, as the Tai Chi flowing through me began to feel like an internal massage, loosening me in many ways.

The Tai Chi practice loosened me while in motion as I surrendered to its flow, and this became the kernel of my Push Hands ability. When my students push on me, there is nothing to push against, I do not contend, I yield. This is the Taoist way. This is the Tai Chi way. All my students see is that I am loose and un-pushable – the *vast journey* that led to this point is unknown, unnamable, and indescribable. That is the way of the Tao.

And all of this, this journey into things too big for me to wrap my head around and comprehend back when I was learning them, had prepared me to let go and flow with the Tao – to open to a reality larger than I could hold, control or understand at any given moment. This whole journey was a lesson in Taoism, and Taoist philosophy helped me comprehend this larger aspect of my Tai Chi and Qigong journey in a way that could affect my entire approach to life.

Why did I spend all of those hours practicing things that made no sense to me? I had a sense that they were leading somewhere to a place I could not conceive of or understand at the time, but I could never have told you this in words in the beginning. I just had feelings that I did not understand, like a heavenly body being pulled in orbit by a force that it does not understand. I had to surrender to a flow that I did not control or direct, even as the world that "made sense," the logical world, the linear world, the busy world of spreadsheets and goals and tangible destinations told me that I was wasting my time on all of this stuff.

This is the way of the Tao. Its rhythms and currents carry us, if we are able to let go of what we think we are, ever toward what we will become. These rhythms often whisper quietly. We have to let go of the world to hear them.

I have come to understand that Tai Chi and Qigong are techniques designed to help us become more subtle, and to unlock us and un-grip us from what is, so that we may unfold into what will become. They can be powerful tools to prepare us to unmoor from the dock and flow with the river toward larger and larger flows and oceans of possibility.

The potential student calling me at the beginning of this chapter, wanting to learn from me how to *push people around*, reminded me where all of my life experience with Tai Chi and Taoism had led. It led me to let go of the desire to push people around and rather unfolded and fed a longing to *let go* and *flow*.

This is the way of the Tao. Lao Tzu explains that the Tao is like water, which is nurturing to all things and never competes with them.

"When you practice Push Hands it should be to help each other to relax ... and to give up the idea of win or lose ... and in doing so both players win."
-- Master Tian Liyang

[quote provided by Belgian Tai Chi teacher, Hilda Cardinaels]

In the beginning of Tai Chi, Qigong, and Nei Gong training, the concept of Qi, or Shen energy is that we have to "create it" or "envision it" to bring it into being.

Over time, we realize that it always exists in endless supply whether we are thinking about it or not. We do not "make Qi," or "control Qi," or "turn on Qi."

Our access to this energy is like a binary computer system, of "1s" and "0s." We have only "two" options: 1) To flip a mental switch causing us to *tighten* and restrict energy's flow, or 2) We can "let go" and "open" to that which *always* existed.

Any mental-Yang attempt to "control it," by its very nature, constricts. The Yin is surrender, and yielding ... and our Yin Tai Chi and Qigong practice can help us discover that whenever and wherever we absolutely "let go," ... the energy expands through and flows through in vast and limitless supply ...

It sounds so simple, and it is. It can take an instant, or a lifetime to comprehend it, if ever.

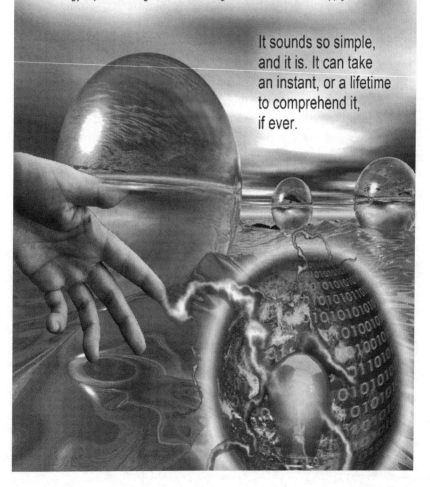

FLOWING WITH THE TAO ...

So you see how Taoism can deeply affect your Tai Chi and Push Hands approach. Taoism also shows how the lessons of Tai Chi can enable us to navigate the Tao. Not just to improve our Tai Chi forms or Push Hands, but to enable us to better navigate the ebb and flow of energy moving through the greater world.

This book will explore the larger ethereal concepts of Taoism in the large long trajectory of our lives and the course of humanity. But, as you saw with the Push Hands chapter, we will also explore practical applications of Taoism in Tai Chi and in our day to day existence.

For example, how does a Tai Chi Taoist drive? If they are living their art, they drive in a Yin yielding way. I was just explaining to one of my students, that before Tai Chi and Taoism, when I drove I thought of "my space" on the road as my domain that should not be violated by another. If someone cut me off, or tail-gated, they had to be flipped off, scolded, or yelled at. I was the defender of order in the world.

Then, over the years of Tai Chi and Push Hands play, and studying the Tao te Ching, I began to let go of my stake in the road. I began to surrender into "the field" of the road or freeway, letting go of myself and opening to a "state of pure awareness" – like we strive for in Tai Chi. In Tai Chi we open to all our sensations without controlling them. When we drop a fork at the table or a coin at a counter, our relaxed body swoops in an effortless way to catch it before it hits the ground, in ways we never could have done without Tai Chi training.

When driving as a Tai Chi Taoist I claim no part of the road. I open to "pure awareness" of the flow, and often note another driver's coming need to switch lanes into mine, even before that driver notices it. I have already either slowed down, sped up, or moved over to allow space for that occurrence before it happens.

There is no "me" when driving as a Tai Chi Taoist. There is only "the flow." My only goal in driving is to support the overall flow of the traffic in the most nurturing way possible. Taking nothing personally, staking no claim, needing no respect. My only desire – becoming one with the flow.

When flowing in the Tao we find we can do the small yet important things in our individual lives more profoundly, like driving, or relating to family. But also, when the Tao or the way of the universe is poised to change the world in big ways, it finds us poised and willing to be a part of that nurturing change. And huge things become possible through us.

I am going to begin this book, like some action thrillers start, with a huge scene from later in the story, in this case beginning with an event that illustrates how the Tao can flow through individuals to literally trigger massive changes throughout the world.

Then, we will go back to the beginning and assemble and unfold how that scene came into being, so that this huge intense scene can make perfect sense to you once you read through the book and get back to it again.

So, we are now going *all the way back* to an excerpt from the 3rd to the last chapter of this book, and if you come out the other side of this wave intrigued by it, we will come back to the beginning, and like action films that use this vehicle, it will all make sense by the time we revisit this scene.

I am going to begin this book, like some action thrillers start, with a brief flash of key insights from later in the story. These insights illustrate how the Tao can flow through individuals to literally trigger massive changes throughout the world. Following these insights, I will share how everything came into being.

Key Excerpts from The Tao of Science, 3rd to the last chapter:

Taoist philosophy is about the connection of all things via a field, an unseen, intangible, nebulous field that permeates all existence. Einstein calls this the "spooky effect," in reference to nonlocality research in physics. When particles are affected or stimulated in some way, particles great distances away would react at precisely the same instant, at speeds "faster than the speed of light." According to known physics, nothing can move faster than the speed of light. In essence, the very fabric of the universe is all connected, which Taoism has understood for thousands of years, long before particle physics came into being.

Research at Princeton University, called The Global Consciousness Project (GCP), found that when humanity focused their minds en masse, it affected computers all across the planet simultaneously. Essentially, electronics were affected by human consciousness. Devices known as Random Event Generators (REGs) were then placed all over the planet. When humanity focused their minds en masse, it caused all of the REGs to go off course. Events which set of the REG's included Princess Diana's death and the World Trade Center collapse.

This suggests that the Taoist view of all beings being connected in a real way was not just flowery poetry, but perhaps actual physics. Physics which they were able to tune into with their consciousness. Einstein himself believed that our feeling of separation was a delusion that we should overcome.

Furthermore, biologist Rupert Sheldrake observed that when rats in a Harvard laboratory suddenly began to learn a maze pattern more quickly, rats in other university studies in Scotland and Australia suddenly also learned the maze more quickly as well.

Then there was my own personal experience with synchronicity and the idea of a group mind. One personal anecdotal synchronous event I experienced made me wonder about the concept of group mind as well. I had traveled to Hong Kong in 2013 and toured the Hong Kong Polytechnic University's Tai Chi Research Laboratory. There I learned that a landmark event had occurred in 1998. A new director took over research and began raising funds to research Tai Chi as part of Chinese Medicine research. This event had global ramifications resulting from papers that would be read by researchers worldwide in universities around the planet.

The year *1998* was also the very first mass Tai Chi and Qigong event, eventually leading to World Tai Chi & Qigong Day in 80 nations. That year was also the very first World Congress on Qigong organized by Dr. Effie Chow, which quickly led to Dr. Effie Chow being appointed by *President Clinton* to the first White House Commission on *Complementary and Alternative* Medicine Policy.

The synchronicity of these 3 events is stunning. 1st being an influential technical university expanding modern scientific research into Traditional Chinese Medical techniques like Tai Chi and Qigong, which would echo through halls of science worldwide via papers they would publish to the researchers worldwide. The 2nd event, a world congress, which would connect said researchers around the global via an annual international conference. And 3rd, a mass global educational event which would train professionals and enthusiasts in Tai Chi and Qigong all over the planet to hold mass public visual events, and utilize those events to gain mass media coverage, and to engage their local and national governments and officials; all to spread this emerging science at a vastly accelerated pace into the global psyche.

A better global plan to advance the spread of Tai Chi and Qigong, and at a time when the world needs it the most, could never have been designed in a Yang linear way. Three people who did not know one another, or have any idea that in different parts of the planet events powerfully augmenting the impact of what they were doing were happening, all being driven to act in their own ways all in the same year, 1998, makes one wonder about the Taoist concept of all life being connected, and the power of letting go of what we are and opening to the Yin, the flow, the unseen rhythms. Could this be an image of the power of the Tao of Tai Chi, could this be an indication of the making of a new science?

As amazing as the above concept is, the heart of Taoist thought does not stop with consciousness and physics research. Taoist concepts also appear to have a real and deep connection with modern Chaos Mathematics "self-replicating theory," which will be discussed later in this book.

I hope that the above blew your mind as much as it did mine, when all of this unfolded in my life. We started with the nebulous and unpredictable Yin, so now we can return to the less unwieldy and more logical Yang--the beginning of this book--to build the case for all of the above. The following chapter presents "The Foundation of Taoism."

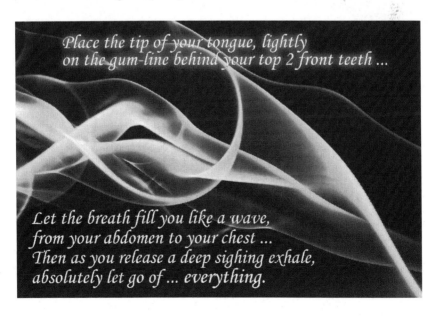

Place the tip of your tongue, lightly on the gum-line behind your top 2 front teeth ...

Let the breath fill you like a wave, from your abdomen to your chest ...
Then as you release a deep sighing exhale, absolutely let go of ... everything.

The Tao ...
does not follow the
logic, and strategies of
normal left brain thinking.

It requires us to let go
of linear thought
and follow the
paths that open
within, throughout,
and all around us,
as they shift
and bend
into all kinds
of directions ...

leading to
destinations
we cannot yet
see or understand ...

THE FOUNDATION OF TAOISM ...

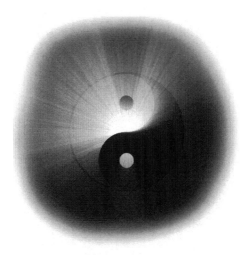

The above image is most popularly known as the Yin Yang symbol, but it is also known as the *Tai Chi* symbol. It is beautifully elegant in its simplicity, because it may be the most complex symbol in human history. To give you an idea of just how complex this symbol is, realize that this 200 plus page book is dedicated to unraveling and unveiling the messages this elegantly simple Tai Chi symbol contains. Yet I can only scratch the surface of its depth in those 200 pages, which just touches the surface of over 40 years of full time exploration on my part.

You will learn how this ancient symbol, as the very heart of Taoist thought and Tai Chi practice, is so profound in meaning that it also relates to quantum physics and cutting edge chaos mathematics in astounding ways. This lovely simple thing people like to wear on earrings or jewelry contains the complexity of the entire universe.

This book also explores how our Tai Chi practice can put us in the very center of the universe, using Taoist concepts to reveal how our Tai Chi practice is the microcosm of our lives. When we hold our Tai Chi forms rigidly, we hold our world tightly. As our Tai Chi forms begin to loosen us over time, our entire lives begin to loosen up around us. More on this later.

Taoists saw the universe as made from the tension, or more accurately the interplay of dynamics, between positive and negative polarities. This is fascinating when you realize that modern physicists see the universe in the same way. Everything, every single thing in the universe is the creation of positive and negative polarities in the form of subatomic particles.

The Taoists use the Tai Chi symbol (above) to illustrate the "Yin" and "Yang," or "negative" and "positive" polarities that make up all of existence:

YIN	YANG
Negative	Positive
Feminine	Masculine
Soft	Hard
Flexible	Rigid
Dark	Light
Cool	Warm
Yielding	Force
Receptive	Dynamic
Repose	Action
Internal	External

Even more fascinating is that over 2,000 years ago, Taoist philosophers understood what modern science just began to comprehend only about 100 years ago. I am referring to the realization that the universe is made not of the solid mass of Newtonian physics, but of energy. Furthermore, the universe is made up mostly of a Quantum Field of empty space or potential energy. Taoists called it the Tao and quantum physicists call it the Quantum Field. This field is a field of non-being, yet all the subatomic particles that make up the universe emerge from this field, a field that in essence is the "mother of all things," as described in the Tao Te Ching. This is how ancient Taoists described the nebulous and unknowable energetic nature of the universe, which they called the Tao.

"If quantum mechanics hasn't profoundly shocked you, you haven't understood it yet. Everything we call real is made of things that cannot be regarded as real."
-- Niels Bohr, Nobel Prize in Physics recipient, 1922
http://www.brainyquote.com/quotes/quotes/n/nielsbohr384378.html

"The Tao that can be told is not the eternal Tao; the name that can be named is not the eternal name. The Nameless is the origin of Heaven and Earth ... All things in the world come from being. And being comes from non-being ... There was something undifferentiated and yet complete, which existed before Heaven and Earth. Soundless and formless, it depends on nothing and does not change. It operates everywhere and is free from danger. It may be considered the mother of the universe. I do not know its name; I call it Tao. "
-- Lao Tzu
http://www.brainyquote.com/quotes/quotes/l/laotzu714975.html
http://www.brainyquote.com/quotes/authors/l/lao_tzu_4.html
http://www.brainyquote.com/quotes/authors/l/lao_tzu_2.html

Our busy daily lives are primarily "yang" energy. But when we slip into the repose of meditative mind-body experiences, we allow "yin" energy to permeate our tight lives. Yin energy loosens. It opens and relaxes us. Tai Chi is designed to make space for the Yin energy to permeate our active lives, because it teaches us how to breathe. It teaches us to loosen, and to open, even when active. The moving Tai Chi forms represent all the normal motions the body is capable of during normal activities. Over time all our actions in life become woven with a meditative mind-body experience of letting go, yielding, and becoming open to flow.

For centuries, Tai Chi and Taoist Philosophy have woven together to form *a way of living*, whereby the principles of Tai Chi or Qigong can be used in our lives. These principles help us to become more aware of the fluid energy dynamics of life, our consciousness, and our unfolding futures that form from our consciousness. The highest purpose of Tai Chi is to find balance between our Yin and Yang aspects, consciousness or being. However, Tai Chi is a Yin art, which makes it the most powerful art in finding balance, because the world is way over balanced with Yang energy and approach. So Tai Chi's Yin approach and development makes it a powerful tool to help the world find balance in all things. This ability to promote balance is a huge thing for the world today. More than ever before in history tools to find balance in our lives are needed. Why?

Our generation is unique among all the millennia of past generations of humanity for 2 reasons:

1st) Our generation is reeling from seeing our global population nearly quadruple in our lifetimes (if you are a baby boomer, like I am). I repeat this because it is such a staggering thing to comprehend. It took all of human history, all those thousands of generations of our ancestors to bring Earth's population up to 2 billion following World War II. Then, in one single generation we are rapidly nearing 8 billion, and may reach 10 billion in my lifetime. The stress and demands this puts on humans explains much of the scourge of modern stress and disease. Stress causes most of the disease in the modern world, according to scientific research.

2nd) We are the children of the technological revolution, and the speed of technological change is doubling every 18 months. I repeat, DOUBLING in speed every 18 months. If you do the math on doubling, then doubling, then doubling, you understand why we all feel constantly 10 steps behind the world, as our computers and smart phone hardware becomes outdated almost before we leave the store. Of course the software updates come even faster.

In order to not just survive in, but thrive in this level of rapid change, humans have to be able to flow and change at a vastly accelerated rate compared to our ancestors, and even our parents. Our children and grandchildren will look back with nostalgia, seeing our harried lives of today as the relaxing *slow* time in history.

Relevant to this is Taoism as a philosophy of change. A seminal book of Taoist principles is the I Ching, the Chinese Book of Changes. Its title speaks for itself.

Understanding all of this leaves one amazed that Tai Chi and Taoism, created hundreds and thousands of years ago, seems to have been created for people today, living in a time of bone crushing change. What I find even more amazing is that this ancient wisdom arrived all around the planet just at the time when it would be most needed. What do I mean by that? Tai Chi and Qigong had been closely held secrets of China for most of history. In fact China really only opened up to the West in the 1970s, during the Nixon Administration. Tai Chi and Qigong began to spread worldwide at that time. But it took decades for the Chinese practitioners who migrated around the world to share and translate them, so that people in those other nations could "get it." Even then, at that time, Tai Chi and Qigong were only available to the few very open minded and dedicated students in those other countries. It really took a couple of generations of teachers, before people in other nations could absorb Tai Chi and Qigong into their lives at a deep organic level. And then to be able to share Tai Chi and Qigong in their own cultural ways, making it accessible to the mass public. Then medical research began in earnest worldwide, as health professionals and medical researchers began to enjoy the benefits of Tai Chi and Qigong. This is what has fueled the rapid spread of these arts throughout the world, as doctors and health publications began telling the public about Tai Chi and Qigong.

To fully appreciate the synchronicity of this, remember that Tai Chi and Qigong are ancient practices, and in all those centuries and millennia, really only China had access to these mind-body arts. Arts which really are the perfect prescription for the times we are in, and the future our generation today faces. But, now, when humanity needs these tools most, in the last 40 years, they have spread to become readily available to nearly everyone on the planet.

My work organizing World Tai Chi & Qigong Day (WTCQD) opened my eyes to this. Had I not worked for 17 years making global connections with teachers worldwide, and seeing photos and videos of WTCQD events from Australia to South America, Africa to Asia, comprising hundreds of events spanning 6 continents — I would have had no idea of how rapidly Tai Chi and Qigong have spread. My training tells me that this is no coincidence. That a nebulous plan has been expanding through individuals all across the planet. Looking back it seems apparent that a grandly and elegantly woven plan, which would have seemed too amorphous and shapeless for any of those involved in it at the time to comprehend, would use those people around the planet in key positions at key moments, to weave this plan together. People who were able to let go of what they were, so they could open to what they would become, and transform the planet as they did. It happened to me. Without being exposed to Taoist concepts of nebulous waves unfolding into larger possibilities for those who surrender to the flow of the Tao, and my constantly allowing Tai Chi to loosen me physically, mentally, and emotionally — I would have been unable to allow my part in this, the formation of a global event, to flow and expand through me. This book is designed to illuminate how the one-two-punch of Taoism as a philosophy, with Tai Chi as a practical experience of Taoist concepts, can very literally serve as a prescription for the future. A prescription that can help us navigate the currents of this coming wave of unimaginable change, that humanity is only just beginning to feel.

[Photo credit, Ahmed Shaaban from Blue Lotus Wellbeing Foundation]

Egyptian World Tai Chi & Qigong Day organizer, Sifu Mohamed Essa, leads WTCQD attendees mass crowd in Qigong movements.

Tai Chi's ability to enable us to "feel the Tao" by loosening our being as we move through our forms, as we move through our lives, prepares us in yet another way for the challenges of the future. We know with emerging science that the planet is all connected; economically, socially, and environmentally. When people suffer in one part of the planet it, often echoes around the world. As when the Asian stock market crashed, all the global indexes responded in kind. When Fukushima Daiichi had its nuclear disaster, radiation went all over the planet, affecting everyone to varying degrees. Coal burning in China or America affects Africa's and Cuba's climate, and on and on.

Being immersed in the sense of flow, that feeling of losing oneself in Tai

Chi and Qigong meditation over and over, day after day, helps us let go of the delusion that we are separate from the world. In fact meditation's effect is evidenced in physical changes in our brain's structure which result in making us feel less isolated. This expanding awareness of the Tao, which Tai Chi and the Internal Arts cultivate, is a powerful and beautiful aspect of the Internal Arts.

World Tai Chi & Qigong Day celebration in Cairo, Egypt, joins with 100s of similar events spanning over 80 nations.

If you are involved in Tai Chi and Qigong in a Taoist way, you are positioned like a surfer gaining footing on his/her surfboard. Poised to *ride* a wave that most of humanity is only standing still at, staring up at it just before it comes crashing down upon them. For you this wave can be fun.

Ladies and gentlemen, I give you *The Tao of Tai Chi* ...

A Yin Yang Teaching Insight ...

When I first began teaching Tai Chi professionally, I was teaching 18 classes a week ...

I was telling the students to "breathe," and to "surrender," and "sink" into their Moving Qigong Meditations or Tai Chi forms. But it was all coming from my head, a Yang action. The tedium of doing this 18 times a week became almost unbearable. It felt so repetitive and contrived over time.

Then, one day I began to "practice what I preached," and when I encouraged students to "breathe" and "let go" and "feel" ... I gave myself space to do it myself ... to surrender into the sensations ...

Since that day I have never had a tedious class again. Moving from Yang control consciousness, to Yin experiential consciousness, *changed everything.* When I let myself flow into that Tai Chi and Qigong freefall into a Zen, or Ch'an meditative experience ... there was only unfolding newness. I surrender to the "wave" of the class, the flow, the Tao of the class, and I am always surprised at how fast the end of the class arrives.

How This Book Came into Being ...

When I began this book I did not intend it to be autobiographical in anyway. I had just intended to include insights I have had over the years, about Tai Chi and Taoist philosophy, ergo the title of this book.

However, as you will be reminded several times in this book, Lao Tzu told us that the Tao that can be spoken of or written of, is not the true Tao. Like currents in the ocean, you can only see how they affect a ship or object caught in the current not the current itself.

So as I began writing, I quickly realized that I would have to share with you my own journey, as an object flowing in the current of the ocean. In this way I can make the Tao more relatable in a meaningful way.

My life, I realized, *is* my Tai Chi Taoist journey, not the things I hold in my head. It is the currents that led me from a small town in Kansas to nations all across the planet. The places where I had extraordinary experiences that defy rational explanation, just as the Tao itself defies rational explanation.

Taoism teaches that all existence that we see in the manifest world is **like a wave** that emerges from the ocean of the Tao, just as a physicist might describe how the particles that make up the manifest world we see emerge from the quantum field. I will share a few events in this book, of when this manifest wave that I am, actually receded back into the ocean of the Tao, back into the field, the ocean from which all existence comes from.

These events — this merging with the field that connects all existence — can happen on some level in Tai Chi and Qigong meditation. You may or may not realize it, but in those moments when we truly "let go" and the Qi flows through our being in the form of our Tai Chi forms and we become so immersed in the experience that for moments we lose our sense of self, forgetting where we are, not thinking consciously — but only feeling *the flow*. This is a glimmer of an experience of receding back into the ocean of all existence. That experience of "losing ones' sense of self and becoming part of the flow," and doing it over and over again in our Tai Chi or meditation practice, makes us feel more connected to the world, to humanity, to life — because this wave that we are is for moments receding back into the field, the Tao, where all things are connected, from whence all things emerge from.

A physical manifestation of this change in ones sense of the world can be seen in neurological research, which shows that for people who meditate regularly their brain functions in ways that leave them feeling less isolated. Another physical manifestation of one's consciousness regularly receding into the field is revealed by research showing that the empathy/compassion parts of our brain get larger — both these brain changes leaving us less isolated and more empathetically connected to others result from regular immersion in the Tao.

But these physical changes in our brain structure, again, are *only shadows* of the light shining through us. Science can see the positive physical effects or shadows this produces, but the constant letting go of the idea of "self" and being so "one with the flow and experience" of our Tai Chi or meditation is more than neurological changes. It is the act of letting go of our grip on the idea of "self," so that the wave we are can recede back into the ocean, the Tao, the field, from whence all things emerge from. So Tai Chi and Qigong meditation can give you glimmers of this experience, and when experienced over and over again, in time, change us profoundly.

But the events I am talking about were a vastly different magnitude. I literally became one with everything — not for just the instants I do during Tai Chi or Qigong meditation, but completely and absolutely one with everything for prolonged periods of time — and nothing was ever the same again. Although some of these events occurred decades ago, it took this long to put it into a readable form, because it took me a lifetime to put all the pieces together, to be able to make sense of it. The following is why I thought now was the time to tell my story.

It seems like just the other day I was one of the young upstarts in the Tai Chi world. And then in the blink of an eye I realized that I was one of the old faces of Internal Arts. You'll understand just how incredibly old I am getting, when I tell you that the famous Kung Fu series was very popular when I was a boy. Not reruns of it, *the actual brand new episodes* which were airing one night a week in the early 1970's.

I was a Kung Fu devotee, but not for the same reason all my friends were. They watched the show for the action, Kwai Chang Caine defending himself in the bar, etc. Of course I thought that was really cool, but it was the scenes in the Shaolin Temple that I looked forward to the most. It was what the old masters said among the stone walls and drifting incense smoke that drew me in. I had no idea what Taoism was, who Lao Tzu was, or that he was the author of the seminal book on Taoism called the Tao te Ching. And I had no idea that the phrases and lessons conveyed to "Grasshopper," the young boy the monks taught in the series, had been derived from the Tao te Ching.

Then I discovered Tai Chi as a young man, about a decade later after leaving university and moving to the city. I started Tai Chi because someone told me it could help with stress. Tai Chi would eventually lead me to the Tao te Ching. It was then that I realized that this was the source of the wisdom I had been drawn to as a boy, so many years before. My eyes glued to our family television screen each week, when it was time for Kung Fu.

I can't really describe to you how excited I was to discover this. That there was a *real ancient philosophy* associated with those scenes I had been mesmerized by, when watching that TV series as a boy. That it wasn't just stuff made up by some TV writer. I spent a lot of time reading the Tao te Ching in those early days of my Tai Chi practice.

Very quickly, I saw how Taoism deeply related to my Tai Chi, and also deeply related to who I was as a being on this planet. It helped me understand how I fit into it, enabling my Tai Chi to evolve into *more than an exercise*, and even more than a philosophy – it enabled my Tai Chi practice to become a way of living. I may not have been able to go live in the Taoist Temple like young Kwai Chang Caine, but I did what I could to live that life, even as I worked corporate jobs and raised small kids. I would spend my break times and lunch breaks at work meditating and doing Tai Chi and Qigong. I was going to Tai Chi or martial arts classes almost every night of the week at that time of discovery. I sought out Alan Watts books and films on Zen, and everything related to Internal Arts that I could get my hands on.

It is fascinating looking back. After being mesmerized by the Taoist Temple scenes in the Kung Fu TV series as a boy, it was years later I would first be told I was going to be a teacher, by a Taoist monk in a Taoist Temple in Hong Kong (more on that fascinating event later).

All of this Internal Arts study, combined with my internal meditations, helped me understand things from the TV series that I could not relate to as a boy, and it was profoundly exciting. In the Kung Fu series one of the old masters, Master Po, had asked young Grasshopper if he could *feel inside his body*. Just as we are invited to do as Tai Chi students, when we practice Gathering Qi, or Universal Post, which are really ancient forms of biofeedback. Essentially listening within ourselves to the subtleties of our being, our most direct access to nature itself. And I would learn over time that this practice attunes us to the subtleties of nature all around us as well.

When the young student in the Kung Fu series had asked the master how he could feel his heart beat, the master had replied that the more important question is 'why can't *you* feel your own heart beat?' The implication being that it is *normal* and natural to be able to feel within, and abnormal not to be able to, even though much of the world would disagree. But, for those of us who have practiced the Internal Arts mindfully for decades, we know that indeed you *can* feel your heart beat. All you have to do is let go of the world outside, and feel within with mindfulness and openness.

Yet for most of us, including myself when I first began my Tai Chi journey, the idea of being able to feel my own heart beat seemed unnatural and impossible, because almost all of my focus was on the world "outside." Not on the universe within. We are taught that this palace of experience within ourselves is not real or important. We are taught that we should ignore the grand ballrooms and libraries and hallways of our internal palace of being. That we should only sit in the attic, looking out the two windows we call our eyes to the world outside, because outside is the real reality. This is what makes the Tai Chi way and the Taoist way different from most of the world's way.

When I heard Master Po talk about feeling your heartbeat so long ago, I too had felt as though the very idea that you could "feel inside yourself" was like magic, and maybe not even real or possible. It is funny now, after 40 years of Internal Arts practice, how it seems just as natural as breathing, or tying your shoes. Today I understand Master Po's being perplexed by the idea that anyone would think that it was impossible to do so. It just feels so normal to me today.

I am even more amazed to hear stories from my students who have only been Tai Chi players for a short time, who awaken to this ability. An older African-American woman in my class a few days ago had been at her doctor's office, getting a checkup. Her blood pressure was very high when a nurse took it. She said she'd told the nurse, "Wait a second, this isn't me, just give me a few moments." She then closed her eyes and breathed Qigong breaths. Letting go of her grip, she opened to the Qi or lightness expanding through her. When the nurse took her blood pressure again, it was 30 points lower, and well within the normal range. When I saw in her eyes how that had amazed her, it reminded me how amazed I was, when I first realized that we can feel inside ourselves and even impact our being with that awareness.

If someone had told me before my journey began that I would one day be able to feel inside myself, and even lower my blood pressure or slow my heart beat at will, I would have thought they were delusional. That is not how our society thinks. We think only someone in a laboratory with a white coat on can create a potion, one we can buy at the drug store that will affect our body. And that this substance's effect can only be understood by a highly trained physician, who will tell us how we feel and how to affect ourselves. Feeling ourselves from the inside and having some influence on what goes on within us is not normal to most people. Just as it was not normal to me before my Internal Arts journey began 40 years ago.

The same is true for feeling the Qi, the energy, our own energetic nature, and thereby attuning to the energetic nature of the universe – the Tao. It is natural to be able to experience these things. They are the flow of nature within us.

Taoism knows that our most direct connection with the world or universe is found by going within. Calming our mind and heart being the first step to calming our body, and ultimately calming our world. It makes such sense to me now after my experiences, but it was not always so. It had to unfold in my life, and Tai Chi was a huge part of that being able to happen.

This is the Taoist journey, and for many Tai Chi players our Taoist journey and our Tai Chi journey become synonymous. If you have not experienced this, well, I guess this is one of the reasons I wrote this book. To perhaps contribute to fostering this union in those who haven't explored it yet. If you haven't, don't take umbrage with my mentioning this possibility. If I had not been open over these 40 years, I would have missed out on some information and experiences that were among the most precious things in my life looking back. I had to be an empty cup in order to allow new possibilities to flow into me. If I continually assumed that as a Tai Chi teacher I had to *already know all there was to know,* I would have been a full cup, incapable of opening to the universes of knowing that would flow to and through me over the years.

I do not want any Tai Chi teacher to think I am saying I know more than you. There are aspects of Tai Chi that you know that I have not been exposed to and could learn from you. Forty years of study in the Internal Arts have shown me that no one single teacher "knows it all," just as no Photoshop user or any sophisticated computer software user "knows it all." If you use Photoshop with an open mind you know that you are always continually learning new tools or techniques about that program from other users you talk to. It is simply too huge, created by too many programmers, for one user to hold all of its possibilities in his/her mind at one time.

I want all teachers to understand my humility before your skills with Tai Chi, so that you will not feel challenged by me sharing my own journey. It is simply my journey, not necessarily "the" journey — yet I think it is a journey worth sharing. One thing it has taught me is that, if we as Tai Chi teachers can continually let go of all we know and be empty and open, the Internal Arts and Taoist philosophy are keys to whole new universes.

Looking back, I wrote this book because I have much to tell after my 60 years on Earth. But the journey that led me here was one of continually emptying and drifting wide eyed and ignorant in a world of newness – experiencing a constant return to child-likeness – following the unfolding path which Lao Tzu described, best followed not by being smart and proud, but by floating, adrift in the world, open mouthed and wide eyed.

Moving Past the "Push Hands Tai Chi Teacher Hitch" ...

When I first began organizing World Tai Chi Day, a Tai Chi teacher from back east emailed me and said, "Man, I have to give you credit. It must not have been easy organizing this event, because organizing Tai Chi teachers is like herding cats."

Tai Chi teachers tend to follow the tune of a different drummer and march to their own beat, following an internal rhythm. Also, Tai Chi is such a huge concept that every teacher has a unique experience with it, and Taoism is an even larger ocean to navigate.

At an NQA (National Qigong Association) Conference a Tai Chi teacher told me and some other teachers a joke I've shared many times over the years. It goes like this: How many Tai Chi teachers does it take to screw in a light bulb? Answer: Only 1, but it takes 99 others to stand around and solemnly shake their heads saying, "That's not the way WE do it."

So we all see different angles of Tai Chi. But this doesn't mean one is wrong and one is right. I heard a story about a group of blind men who had never heard of an elephant before, all feeling the elephant between them. One wraps his hands around the animal's trunk, and exclaims, "An elephant, it feels like a water hose!" Another man has the tail, and states, "It is like a whisk broom." Another man feels a leg and says, "It is like a pillar or column." All are correct, and if they put their heads together, they can get a much clearer picture of what an elephant is.

The thing that keeps Tai Chi teachers and enthusiasts from "putting our heads together" is the "hitch."

I think most Tai Chi teachers have experienced that "hitch," that moment of tightness we feel when exposed to new concepts or insights about Tai Chi, that have not been part of our personal experience. It is because we fear that these new insights challenge what we know, what we've learned. This is human nature. Neurologists have actually located the part of the brain that causes us to brace against and auto-reject new information.

In Push Hands, I flow in ovals toward and away from my student, and at a point I feel a "hitch," a resistance. This resistance is when they are tightening and vulnerable, because they are resisting — and often this resistance they hold is unbeknownst to them. I have to point it out to them, and help them breathe and let go around it, to allow that hitch to melt away — and I can see in their eyes that sometimes they only really become aware of it at the moment they feel it let go and feel it disappear.

These physical patterns of holding on and resisting are not just physical, as seen in Tai Chi and Push Hands practice. They are also emotional and mental. Taoism is a method of "understanding" resistance and flow, while Tai Chi and Qigong are methods for "feeling" resistance and flow. Together, they are a powerful learning method that takes you way beyond linear left-brain book learning.

Breathe, let go, be open to the flow. This is the Tai Chi way, the Taoist way. I invite you to ride the current of this book and see how it flows into your journey's current.

As we relax, and "sink" into our Tai Chi forms, letting the power flow through our loose body, we are practicing a Yin way in a very tangible physical manner. Taoist philosophy gives us a way to see how this practice of "opening to the flow" and loosening around it in our Tai Chi practice, becomes not just an exercise, but *a way of life*. Tai Chi becomes a model for a way of living more powerfully and effortlessly in all our interactions, not just when we are playing Tai Chi. Chinese people don't say they are going to "work out," they say they are going to "play" Tai Chi. This can be a model for how we approach every aspect of life.

Release Ambition, The Art of Faith, Science & Surfing ...

The masters in the Kung Fu series implored Grasshopper to free himself from ambition, to let his only goal in life be to flow with the Tao. My life has shown me that we can do extraordinary things when we allow the currents of the Tao to carry us. It has not amassed me great wealth, which unfortunately is often the measure of success in today's popular culture (and probably always has been). I have found that only when I let go of ambition can I do huge things. When my goal is solely profit my mind and heart and field constrict, and I can feel the flow of Qi and the current of the Tao being restricted like a dammed river.

I have made a living teaching Tai Chi, but it has almost always been hand to mouth, requiring me and my wife and my family to have faith, letting the stones appear as our foot neared the water. To do Tai Chi well, we have to do it loosely, and to do it loosely, we have to have faith. If we fear we tighten. Albert Einstein once said that the most important question we can ask ourselves is: "Is the Universe a friendly place?" All of our paths in life flow from that answer. I have come to think of Tai Chi as "faith walking," because answering Einstein's question affirmatively lessens fear, and loosens our Tai Chi forms. This is the high goal of Tai Chi – loosening around our forms.

You may not have expected to read Einstein quoted in a book on Tai Chi and Taoism, but you will see his name several times, as you will also see how I believe Taoism to be a high science in the next chapter.

Lao Tzu offered a vision of the fabric of the universe and our being that would be validated by modern quantum physicists thousands of years after Lao Tzu's creation of the Tao te Ching. Over my lifetime I have seen how each year technology evolves, expanding science's ability to understand what was not understandable before, making this Tai Chi and Taoist journey become ever more fascinating through my lifetime. My appreciation of the depth of Tai Chi and Taoist insights of Chinese culture has opened and deepened, as technology validates ancient concepts.

For example, in this book you'll learn how Tai Chi led me to a year of acupuncture training. This revealed to me how modern technology now validates the existence of acupuncture points on the body, points mapped out thousands of years before electronics and electronic detection devices existed. Later, you'll also read how I discovered that aspects of Feng Shui, the Chinese art of architectural energy flow, are actually grounded in physics, health and psychological science. Again and again over the years I have seen how ancient Chinese concepts once thought to be un-scientific, actually turned out to be a high science that modern Western science is only now beginning to catch up with.

My generation of Internal Arts teachers has had the opportunity to see things that were thought of as "mystical," when we began our journey nearly a half century ago, now becoming accepted scientific thought. No generation of Tai Chi and Qigong teachers in our long history have seen what we have seen, where the Taoist and Tai Chi Yin worlds have begun to come together with the Yang scientific analytical world, as science validates Internal Arts concepts of the mind and body.

I personally have had the rare opportunity of being right at the heart of this amazing event in human history due to my experiences. For 25 years I have taught in major medical centers and halls of modern science, where physician's lives were changed by Tai Chi and Qigong. They became obsessed with seeking out all the scientific studies they could find about Tai Chi and passing them on to me. However, these four decades of study of Tai Chi and Taoism goes beyond just physical health science catching up with Tai Chi. It goes far beyond even that profound journey of discovery and awakening.

Lao Tzu, the father of Taoist philosophy, tells us that the universe beneath the surface of the manifest world is a flow of energy (incidentally, modern physicists also tell us the manifest world is made of energy, which I discuss in more detail later).

Taoist philosophy explains that if we can turn within and learn to *let go,* we can be open to a sense of those currents and flow toward the ever evolving being that we are continually becoming. And toward the ever evolving world our becoming is creating – the way a surfer is washed on the waves of the ocean when they surrender to the power of the wave, and stop fighting it or trying to control it. Both surfers and Taoists attune to the rhythm of the waves beneath the surface.

I was a Kansas boy living in Southern California when I began Tai Chi, and first studied the Tao te Ching, and was learning how to body surf for the first time. The parallels of the images Lao Tzu conveyed about surrendering ourselves to the currents of the universe became demanded of me on a physical level, when I was caught in those sometimes very large waves, in the famous surf of Huntington Beach, where I lived at the time. When you receded into one of those large waves, you learned very quickly that if you *tightened up* and resisted, the wave would drive you down into the beach, and you would be hammered by the overwhelming power of the tide. You would come up sputtering, gasping for breath, with sand in your pants and maybe even some scrapes. However, when you finally learned to "let go" and "surrender yourself" to the wave, you would have a very exciting ride in the swirling currents, and then emerge quite unscathed as the wave passed.

This became a model for my Tai Chi and for my life, this letting go and surrendering to the flow. But I don't think this would have happened for me without the Tao te Ching's influence in my life. It enabled me to see these parallels of the power beneath the shimmering crystalline blue waves of the mighty Pacific Ocean, and the waves and currents beneath the visible universe that Lao Tzu attempted to describe in his poetry. It flowed through me when I surrendered to the constant changes of my Tai Chi forms. The Tao te Ching gave me a reference or context for my Tai Chi experience, but also for all other events that happened in my life. In the end, Tai Chi, Qigong, and Taoism were not so much attempts to learn something I had never experienced before. Rather it was the study of these arts and sciences of the body and mind, which were my attempt to make sense of things that had been happening to me for many years before. Things that modern Western culture had not prepared me for.

I had felt adrift. I was experiencing insights and events beyond modern Western scientific explanation. Taoism and Tai Chi were the life lifelines my flailing hands grasped onto, pulling me to see a new order, to see patterns in what had felt like chaos. Even as Taoism helped me see order in chaos, Tai Chi helped me feel more calm and at home in change and chaos. When we start learning Tai Chi it often feels chaotic to move four limbs in four different ways, while trying to breathe full breaths, be aware of our Vertical Axis, keep our shoulders relaxed, and more. Then over time it all begins to feel more natural, and it teaches us that we can relax into chaos. That the disturbance chaos causes in us will pass when we breathe and relax.

Tai Chi's essence, according to top Tai Chi experts that I have talked to, and from my own experience, is learning to let go, to let a flow pass through us and carry us through our movements and the changes of life. As amazing as the mounting medical science is, showing how Tai Chi can prevent or treat most major illnesses, it is only a reflection of the power of Tai Chi, not the actual power of Tai Chi. This emerging scientific validation and data on Tai Chi is hugely important and will change the world in vast ways.

But the *true power* of Tai Chi is what happens within the Tai Chi player and to his/her world. This process of opening to a flow that cannot be controlled and cannot be named, but can only be experienced. The fact that the medical data showing how Tai Chi and the Internal Arts can save society trillions of dollars in health costs in the future, is only the "reflection" of this power. It is a testament to just how enormous Tai Chi is. Taoist philosophy can be a powerful guide or map to help open doors of the mind and heart, to expand the Tai Chi players' boundaries of possibility in their Tai Chi and Internal Arts study.

The Yang everyday world operates in four dimensions; longitude, latitude, altitude, and time. If you know those four things about anything, you can locate it on the planet, which is how our world operates. The Tao operates in planes and realms beyond that, which is what this book explores. Showing in real life examples how the Tao's roadmap is more of a roadmap for "letting go of destinations," and opening to ones larger than we can comprehend. Tai Chi can be a vehicle to practicing this art.

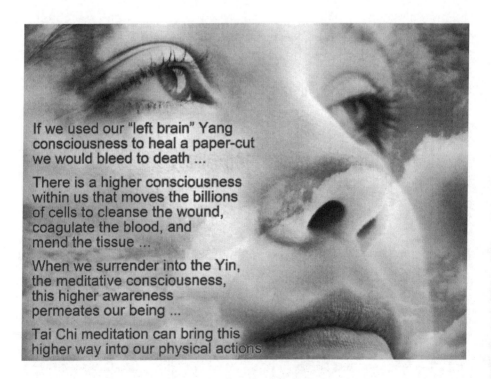

If we used our "left brain" Yang consciousness to heal a paper-cut we would bleed to death ...

There is a higher consciousness within us that moves the billions of cells to cleanse the wound, coagulate the blood, and mend the tissue ...

When we surrender into the Yin, the meditative consciousness, this higher awareness permeates our being ...

Tai Chi meditation can bring this higher way into our physical actions

Taoism: Practical Self-Help, or World Changing Vision ...

All this airy talk of the Tao and its rhythms can make us feel obtuse and thick as we try to wrap our heads around what is too big to fully grasp. When first reading the Tao te Ching, my head would sometimes get tight trying to figure out something that my life experience hadn't given me the context for. So here's a tangible example of flowing with the Tao, that our left-brain can get its arms around.

Today I was pulling up to a signal light. I thought I might turn off the main street and find my way over to another street, one that was more green and scenic. Either path would lead to the store I was driving to. Then the left turn signal turned from green to yellow, and the opposite traffic began to move. I couldn't turn left as I had originally planned, so I gave up the idea of a nicer drive to my destination. I just took a breath and let go of all of it. Until the traffic started in my lane. It then all became so clear to me. I realized that if I changed into the left lane at that moment, the opposite traffic would have passed by then. The road would be clear and would lead directly to the more scenic road I sought. It all became so clear and effortless. The timing was perfect because I had let go of my grip on my original plan, and just opened to the changes. I hit almost every green light on my way to where I wanted to go, and it all just felt so right and effortless.

Now, you may think all this was coincidence and not really an example of the Tao. So forget about it literally being an example of flowing with the Tao, and look at it like a metaphor, simile or allegory, of Flowing with the Tao "in a tangible life way."

Flowing with the Tao can happen in these little moments of our daily lives. But I also look back at how I became an art major at the university, then lost interest after a year. I then switched to sociology, eventually learned Tai Chi, and then became a payroll administrator. Following that I then became a political activist, community organizer, media coordinator, and voter registration and campaign staffer – all of which eventually prepared me to one day found World Tai Chi & Qigong Day. Had I tightened up and held onto any one of those careers, and not listened or felt the flow that pulled me to the next wave of experience, I would not have been prepared to do that larger task when the time arrived. There is no way to plan for this. Each of these career changes was necessary to absorb, to enable me to organize a world event one day. But letting go of each one, once what was needed was absorbed, was the key.

Looking back, I see how the waves carrying me on their tides led to a center. It was like a spinning vortex, that seemed like swirling chaos, but was actually always pulling me toward a destination where all the swirls would come together. An elegant process that has been building for nearly 60 years. It began with ethereal experiences I and my wife had when we were children in 1963, and culminating with our pioneering Tai Chi and Qigong into modern healthcare, corporate wellness, education, penal rehabilitation and more. It put us in a position via our Tai Chi book published worldwide, to organize a world event and spark teachers worldwide to expand Internal Arts into society at a vastly accelerated pace.

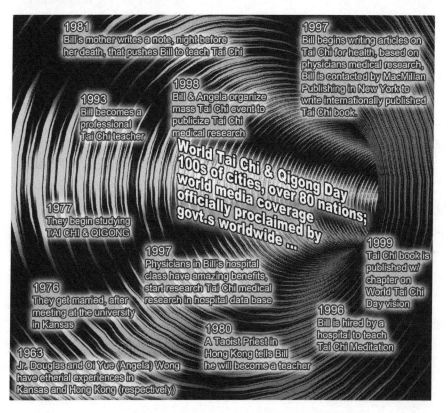

"Our Tai Chi programs continue to grow and our numbers of Tai Chi Schools continue to grow at a phenomenal rate and I feel your efforts are fueling this growth worldwide and we are all in awe of what the World Tai Chi & Qigong Day has done."
-- Dave Pickens, National Chairman Chinese Martial Arts Division United States Amateur Athletic Union

---

I do not think that I and my wife are unique in getting nudges from the Tao, to help us toward a destiny where we can most contribute a nurturing verse to the universal poem. I don't think the challenge is "getting the nudges," I think our challenge is to become quiet enough, subtle enough, to recognize them when they come to us — and loose enough to allow the waves to flow through our lives.

A Taoist Tai Chi Exercise:
When you drop your Duck's Beak for Single Whip have your partner/student/teacher grab your wrist and wiggle your arm to see if you "hold" your arm, or if you surrender to their wiggling of your arm.

The goal: to practice yielding and surrender

The above Taoist Tai Chi Exercise looks easier than it is. If you are like me, when you try it, you will find that you are "holding on" more than you think.

I found that I had to breathe deep Qigong breaths, and let every cell of my body – my arm, shoulder, and back – "exhale" and "let go," again and again, to become supple enough to allow my arm to go into a freefall wiggle when my student shook my arm. To have this revealed after 40 years of Tai Chi training was *humbling*.

The Yin, Internal Art, of Tai Chi play gives us a vehicle to play at "allowing" the flow to pour through us, not just to improve our Tai Chi method, but to also enable us to mentally, emotionally, and physically allow the Tao's currents to flow through our lives.

Taoism: A Portal to a Deeper Experience of Truth ...

Lao Tzu explains that this journey toward the Tao, which ultimately has become my Tai Chi journey, is deep and ever unfolding. One we can only take by *letting go* of control and being open to experiences larger than we can comprehend. As huge as Tai Chi's unfolding is, the concept of the Tao, the way of the universe, is much deeper and wider. In time you begin to find that Tai Chi all along was a portal through which you could experience the Tao, the way of the universe.

I have been on this journey for nearly 55 years. It has shown me that the Taoists were absolutely correct. The world we see, this manifest world, is only the tiny tip of the iceberg of reality. There is a vast existence just beneath the surface of what we call reality, and given the right circumstance, the right moment, it can reveal itself if we are open to it. When we become aware of the Tao, the energetic nature of the universe, we can never go back to where we were, who we were. Or to the smaller world we thought was the totality of existence before.

My study revolved around Sociology at the university at first, and then to Tai Chi and Qigong, Taoism. Later this journey led me to seek a layman's grasp of Quantum Physics and Chaos Mathematics. None of this was for the purpose of "being smart," or impressing people. Rather it was a personal desire to make some sense of the vast experiences and insights I had during my life. Experiences that made no sense in the way I had been raised to make sense of the world.

My Tai Chi journey has become in the end, not an attempt to learn something new, so much as it has become a lifelong attempt to understand and make sense of awakenings that occurred before and after discovering Tai Chi. For me, Taoist philosophy was an expansion and facilitator of Tai Chi's ability to *unveil truths* that had *always* existed within me, not because of Tai Chi or Taoism – for the truths had *always existed* deep within reality.

Later in this book I will explain how and why Taoism is not a religion, but rather a clarifying tool. If your religion or faith is the truth of the universe, then Taoism is the cloth that will help you clean your glasses, in order to see your truth with even greater clarity.

Tai Chi and Taoism are tools to cleanse the central nervous system, including the brain. With fresh clean circuitry you can behold the truth of the universe. Taoism does not tell you what that truth is, it only cleans the lenses of your glasses for you.

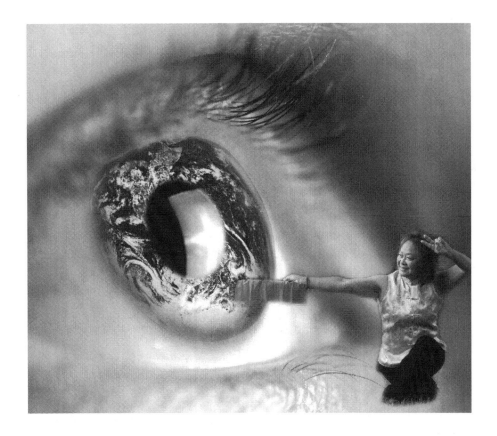

The Simplicity of Complexity -- The Center of the Universe

Centuries ago Galileo was persecuted for advocating the theory that the Sun, and not the Earth, was the center of the universe. Once that reality was accepted it enabled science to understand a plethora of other realities.

Taoists have been derided for declaring that, not the world, but rather that "we" are the center of the universe. They understood that the physical universe, the sub atomic structure which science works to explain, is most immediately and prominently experienced *within us*. WE are the stuff of the universe, and it can be experienced within, as well as being experienced through an electron microscope, or a particle accelerator.

Taoism teaches that within us exists "the entire universe." I know this is true, and not because I read it somewhere or figured it out through my studies. I know because I have felt it, I have experienced it in the most tangible and visceral way – and it shattered the way I saw the world. As my old world broke apart a vast new awareness of something deep and profound discovered space to expand through me. I began to see how precious we are, how precious all life is. Because we are, each and every one of us, connected to ALL LIFE. In feeling that reality it revealed to me just how profound and sacred every being, every life, and every single moment is.

Tai Chi and Taoism at their highest are about "being in the moment," fully experiencing all the sensations our being has to offer at any given moment. When we are present in Tai Chi, we fully sink into our stance. Our balance is far more secure, our reflexes are more instant, our sense of self and dexterity more acute. The movements flow through us in more powerful and expansive ways when we sink and surrender completely into each Tai Chi movement, rather than holding back or holding on. Tai Chi can be a model to loosen our psyche for other larger insights and enlightenment. It won't be Tai Chi or Taoism that give those insights, it will be the true nature of the universe that gives them. Tai Chi and Taoism can simply help loosen us up on all levels, so that we are open when these flows of insight are ready to expand through us.

Tai Chi is a Yin art, yet it is a constant flow between Yin and Yang, preparing, or positioning for a movement (Yang), and then sinking or surrendering into it (Yin). This is a model for life, loosening, flowing between the interplay of the Yin and Yang forces, between the action and yielding.

In the beginning, Tai Chi movements feel like Yang, or action. But, as we practice them over and over, and they become a part of us ... it begins to feel as though we are "surrendering" into them, our actions become a Yin, yielding, surrender to "a flow" passing through us ...

The moments that have revealed the nature of the universe have not happened when I was actually doing Tai Chi or Qigong. But in some instances I do believe that the Internal Arts prepared me physically, mentally, emotionally, and energetically, to be able to open to these events and experiences when they did happen. A golfer who won a big tournament was being interviewed on television, and was asked about how his practice contributed to his victory. The golfer said he had found that his performance that day had little to do with his practice the day or week before. He said that today's performance was more of a reflection of the practice he had done two weeks or three weeks before.

We cannot demand insight and awakening. Tai Chi and Qigong cannot turn it on like a light switch in our home. But, our training of practicing "letting go," and allowing effortless motions to flow through us as we relax out of the way. It can prepare us so that when some cosmic window opens and the waves of the Tao find a space to flow through us, we can let go. We can surrender, and we can be washed on their tides. We will not own them or control them if this happens, but we will be changed by them. Our Tai Chi play will never be the same again, nor will anything about us or our world be the same.

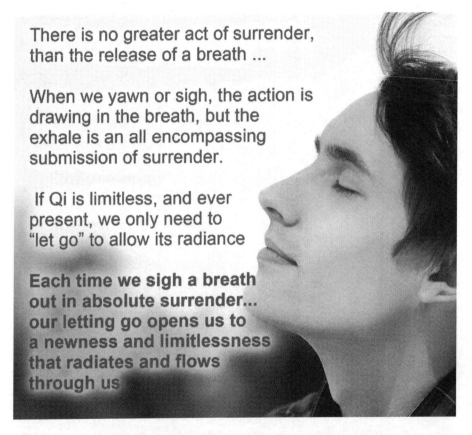

There is no greater act of surrender, than the release of a breath ...

When we yawn or sigh, the action is drawing in the breath, but the exhale is an all encompassing submission of surrender.

If Qi is limitless, and ever present, we only need to "let go" to allow its radiance

Each time we sigh a breath out in absolute surrender... our letting go opens us to a newness and limitlessness that radiates and flows through us

Bruce Lee wrote that we should learn all we can about our arts, and then try to forget everything we learned so that a raw organic spontaneity can flow through us. Lao Tzu told us that we have to let go of what we think we are, so that we can be open to becoming what is trying to unfold through us. If I had to summarize Tai Chi, Qigong, and the Internal Arts into minimal words, I would call them *The Art of Letting Go* – and this is what Taoism is. It sounds much simpler than it is. Yet, when looking back, it *is* that simple, the simplest thing in the world. A wise man once wrote that 'truth is always simple, but humanity will always stampede all over simple truth trying to get to something more complicated.'

I don't want to sound superior, as if I am above this tendency to stampede over simple truth to get to something more complicated. I too often dismissed the profound because of its simplicity. My Tai Chi began as striving for complexity, but over time it evolved into a Taoist journey, a journey of letting go of the allure of complexity. Yet paradoxically, in surrendering to the flow of elegant simplicity one finds oneself opening to complexity far beyond what the linear left-brain consciousness could ever juggle or comprehend.

Lao Tzu told us that it will seem as though we are doing nothing when we are getting all things done. Tai Chi, Qigong, and Taoism are high sciences designed to help us untangle the complexity of our lives and our world. As you'll read in these pages, they offer vastly profound solutions to the world's problems, yet are simple and elegant.

After nearly 20 years of being a global advocate of spreading Tai Chi and Qigong throughout society at all levels (through education, corporate wellness, senior care, drug and penal rehabilitation, etc.), I have come to find that *our biggest challenge or hurdle,* in getting the institutions of the world to see the vast import of Tai Chi and Qigong, is their *elegant simplicity.*

If you ever watched the HBO series Silicon Valley, you may have laughed at how the heroes of the show are so frustrated to find that their product, their new state of the art algorithm that makes data loading many times faster for users, fails to become popular. The reason it doesn't become popular isn't because it is not a profound leap forward in technology. It fails because it IS a profound leap forward in technology. The public cannot wrap its head around their product because it is so much more advanced, elegant and simple than what the public is currently used to.

This group's frustration is something that all of us who know the true societal potential of Tai Chi have felt for many years (as a solution to many social problems). The Tai Chi and Taoist world has been waiting hundreds of years for humanity to be able to wrap their heads around this "new technology." A technology that is hundreds of years old.

Why People Laugh at the Tao …

Lao Tzu explained that if it were not laughed at, it would not be the true Tao.

When the uninitiated person watches us flow through our Tai Chi movements, higher minds may see beauty and peace. However, others see only a person moving arms, legs, hands and feet in funny ways that make no sense. They have no concept of the depth of what we feel. The rhythms of our breath, our sensations, our loosening and flow that massages our being as we let Tai Chi flow through us. They have no concept of how helper T cell counts are being elevated, our blood pressure is being normalized, our respiratory system is becoming more effective, or how our balance and proprioception are being vastly improved. Nor do they know how our brains are being physically enlarged, and how the very fabric of our physical being, our DNA strands, are being healed as we flow through these "silly" movements they watch us perform.

This is a microcosmic glimpse of the Tao, and the vastly undervalued experience of it. Tai Chi can become a key to unlock the gate to the garden of the Tao, for those Tai Chi players who wish to experience that expanded state. But ultimately, you will understand that just as Tai Chi was a key to open a gate to the Tao, that Taoism was just a key to open you to the flow, the way of the universe. Which is nebulous, and cannot be named or held within any exercise or philosophy. Just as an ocean current cannot be contained or held, it can only be felt as it passes or is ridden to a destination.

In this book you will read about events in my life that you may think of as *miracles*. But what 40 years of being in the heart of the Internal Arts movement has shown me, as it has flowed into the halls of medical science, is that often what we think of as "mystical" at one point, becomes provable science one, two or three decades later. Human consciousness is in constant evolution and expansion, as is our technological ability to expand science's understanding of the inner and outer universe. Universes that become more amazing and more vast, as our ability to understand them expands.

My reality, and the reality of millions around the world who have practiced the Internal Arts for decades, has long been larger than sciences' ability to validate it. Then we see in our lifetimes how science catches up, suddenly able to measure brainwave changes, neural changes, immune system improvement, the energetic emanations of Qi and more. What we have felt and knew to be true in our own experience for years, but had to wait for science to validate at a later time, as evolving technology enabled that validation.

We are the first generation, in all the thousands of years of Qigong and hundreds of years of Tai Chi evolution, to have this experience. We are the children of the technological revolution; no other generation has seen such advances in such a short amount of time as we have. And those of us involved in the Internal Arts have had an experience no other Tai Chi or Qigong player in history has been able to witness – science validating what was once considered mystical when we first were exposed to it.

Some of what I will reveal of my journey in this book, I will attempt to explain with the science and philosophy that I have gathered in my long journey, in my own personal quest to help me understand or explain what has happened to me. But some of what you read, of some of the experiences I have had, I cannot explain. It does not mean that they were not real. They were, and really happened to me. Some may not believe me, and I have no control over that. All I can do is tell you my true story and let you do with it what you will.

This book may stretch you. The experiences in my life that created it certainly have stretched me far past the point I would have ever dreamed could be possible.

I hope you enjoy this Tai Chi Taoist journey. I hope you enjoy being stretched, loosened and opened. It is the way of the Tao. It is the way of Tai Chi.

TAOISM IS NOT A RELIGION ...

"To those who yield all power, great power becomes available. That is the way of the Tao.
That is the way of Tai Chi.

To those who let go of their grip on knowledge
limitless knowledge flows through like a river.

Do not *try* to yield, just *let go*, it is the opposite of effort.

Let go of trying to put truth in a box and worrying about giving it names.
As mathematicians know, a set cannot contain itself. It is folly to try.

Our words are the set. Words are the fence of containment and control.
Experience beyond words cannot exist within those fences.

Allow space. Open minds do not grip, they open and flow.
In letting go, great expanding truths have space to lilt through the ether of consciousness.

There is no good truth or bad truth. Truth is truth. We can only open, or close ourselves.

Truths do not require us to grip them in our heads and bodies to make them real.
Truth is truth. It is and always will be, we do not need to grip it or fear it."
-- Taoist allegory

Over 40 years of Tai Chi study, and nearly 20 years working with Tai Chi teachers around the world, on rare occasions I have encountered Tai Chi teachers who tightened up, and refused to consider Taoist thought because they believed it challenged their religion. So I felt compelled to start with this chapter, to quell those concerns, because Taoist philosophy, a philosophy and not a religion, is the very heart of Tai Chi.

I have come to see Taoism and Tai Chi, and Qi, or life energy, as a hybrid of philosophy and high science. A hybrid trying to understand and make tangible the energetic nature of our being and the universe within, throughout, and all around us. Taoism does not compete with any religion. Its examination of reality is no more heretical to religion than is a physicist, astrophysicist or botanist, looking at the workings of life, the world, and the universe. Taoism, like all sciences, is a study. It is a search for truth, attained by observing the natural world, including our own consciousness which is a part of the natural world.

For the record, I consider myself a Lutheran Christian, although I am quick to add that I have found great wisdom in all religions and spiritual insights from around the world. I also completely respect the position of agnostics and atheists as well.

The reality is that Qi, or life energy, flows or radiates through us and through all living things. I feel this energetic nature of my being and of the universe as a physical sensation. It is as real as the air I breathe, and anyone who quiets and attunes to their subtle awareness will feel it in time. The energetic nature of the universe is fact, it is not religious dogma. The flows and expanses of energy beneath the surface of the manifest world is fact which can be experienced, a fact that we can acknowledge, or a fact that we can fear and close off to, and be willfully ignorant of. But it does not make those currents of energy or the Tao go away, it just means we choose to be ignorant of it.

If a surfer or a sailor chooses to be ignorant of the tides and currents of the ocean they float or ride upon they are in for one very tough ride/life. The Tao is the tide of the universe we all ride upon. It is not a religious dogma, it is a science that modern science has not come to grips with – *yet*. It will one day.

Chaos mathematicians and quantum physicists are at work trying to understand patterns and depths of our reality that are not yet understandable. But I predict that as science's understanding of our universe deepens, as neurology and psychology, sociology and other physical and social sciences and fields of study evolve, in time will increasingly validate the Taoist understanding of our nature. Of our connection to the field that connects all things. So do not fear that you are betraying your religion or your God, or your traditions, when you walk into Taoist philosophy and Tai Chi's deeper experience with an open mind and open heart.

Look back at history and you will see that again and again, from Galileo to Abu Bakr Muhammad ibn Zakariy Rz, from Michael Servetus to Albert Einstein, and to Michelangelo, minds that reached beyond the norm were considered heretical. These men were simply being open minded and seeing deeper realities. Whether it be that the Earth rotates around the sun; or the medical internal realities of the human body; or larger social beliefs on pacifism, they were looked at with suspicion because they saw a deeper reality than society at the time did. There was nothing to fear from what they were observing, for they were only observing truth. Truth is not dangerous and God has nothing to fear from truth.

If Taoism is a high science, which it is, then it is worth looking back at historical patterns of not yet accepted science which was viewed with suspicion, and even resulting in the persecution of visionaries.

One very poignant example is Michelangelo's famed Sistine Chapel painting, of God's finger touching Adam's finger with the spark of life. This is a perfect example, because it was the result of Michelangelo performing autopsies on cadavers for years since he was 17. Human autopsy was forbidden by the church at the time. Looking at the physical reality of the human body and the human brain was forbidden. Michelangelo considered himself a Christian who was curious about the physical nature of the universe. Just as most scientists today, according to polls, consider themselves religious. They see no conflict between their yearning to understand physical creation and their religion.

Michelangelo also explored the realms of human consciousness with the same scientific curiosity. This too was then forbidden by the church. In his Sistine Chapel painting he installed a secret message that would not be discovered until in our lifetime. When a neurologist from the United States, staring up at the Chapel ceiling while on holiday in Italy, realized that Michelangelo had painted the human brain, the *right brain* more specifically. This was very significant, that this perhaps most iconic artistic rendering of human connection with spiritual consciousness, was actually an image of the human "right brain."

Michelangelo, a devout Catholic, had been a meditator, a student of the Jewish Kabbalistic traditions, a mystical meditative aspect of Judaism, which understood that the meditative states were considered a right brain experience. I'll get into this more in this book, but the left brain is considered our analytical side because thoughts are formed into words in the left brain verbal center. Before thoughts and experiences are defined in this linear way, they flow in a meditative experience of right brain nebulous and open consciousness. This is the meditative state, where the brain is saturated in Alpha brain waves, a state of consciousness that neurologists have found mind body Internal Arts promote. The breath and physical motions and sensations becoming a type of meditation mantra occupying the mind, to allow brain wave shifts.

Michelangelo was a devout Christian, but was also a man of science, who sought to understand the true nature of physical reality. This included the realms of human consciousness and the inner ethereal aspects of reality, which he pursued via his study of the Jewish Kabbalah's meditative mind-body arts. Today we can appreciate his open minded efforts to understand reality, and call him a visionary. But, had his activities been known publicly at the time, he would have been persecuted as anti-Christian and as a heretic. He was a man of science, and this is a good lesson for anyone who looks at the Chinese philosophy and science of Taoism with suspicion. Fear not, truth is truth, there is no evil truth or good truth. There is simply truth. You can look at a truth and understand that truth, or you can turn away from it and suppress it and hide from its reality. But reality does not go away any more than the ocean currents go away if a sailor or surfer refuses to acknowledge their existence.

Again, this Taoist insight into the energetic nature of our being and the universe is not mysticism, this is physics. Taoism, Tai Chi, Qigong, and Qi have long been thought of as mystical, but I have come to see them as "science that the technology of our scientific method has not caught up with yet." When I began studying the Internal Arts and learning Nei Gong energy meditations, science had not caught up with Qi. Today however, advances in technology have enabled science to detect aspects of the energy emitted from human beings, or what the Chinese masters would have called Qi. Consider this. If you had shown a caveman a remote TV controller, he may well have thought "spiritual influences," or even "evil spirits" were involved. Funny? Yes. But today, although fewer and fewer all the time, there are still a few people who do not understand the science of Taoism or Tai Chi. They jump to the conclusion that something "religious" is involved, something they have to be scared of. The way the caveman may have reacted to the remote TV controller he did not yet understand. Pointing his bony finger of suspicion at the TV remote as he jumped up and down hysterically in fear of the evil device, that can change pictures magically.

When one allows the Qi to flow through, performing external Qigong, they are allowing subtle energies to flow through them and out their hands into another being. Research shows this can calm the tissues, help reduce swelling and edema, foster less damage from trauma and more rapid healing, and leave the patient "feeling better." One person, perhaps a Michelangelo, might look at this and wonder what is physically happening in the mind and hands and body. While another person may jump up and down and point suspiciously at the External Qigong practitioner, and exclaim that something evil is going on. At this point, we each must decide which role we want to assume. My point here is that there is nothing to fear.

If you can let go of any resistance to Taoist concepts, it will free you and your Tai Chi, to freefall into deep oceans of possibility. Taoism's understanding of the energetic nature of the universe, which any physicist will now tell you is scientific fact (the energetic nature of the universe, that is), really makes Taoism not mysticism at all, but again, more of a hybrid of science and philosophy.

Chaos mathematics is a new science that is unraveling deeply complex aspects of reality, trying to understand living systems. Old math could only study closed systems, a flow in a pipeline for example, but could never attempt to conceive of the complexity of a stream with its swirling eddies and innumerable branches and irregularities. Chaos mathematics tries to understand complex systems like human activity and weather, using vastly complex computer models, in order to view huge amounts of data in concise ways that enable researchers to see huge patterns in reality. A reality that mathematicians of old would never have been able to comprehend.

Chaosticians are able to do this by translating vast amounts of mathematical calculations into a conceivable image known as "fractal art." If you've seen the beautiful and complex images of fractal art, those organic images stick with you forever. Some call them the mathematical representation of the fingerprint of nature.

In time, Chaos mathematics and Taoist concepts of vast repeating patterns of reality will come closer together. Just as we now know mystical insights of ancient meditators look increasingly like modern quantum physicists' insights, into the underlying energetic nature of the universe.

Observe how the smaller fractal tip, when enlarged, looks like the larger fractal wings, the way a leaf's veins look like the tree it came from.

Taoism is a science of internal research to try to experience and understand the unfolding patterns of the mathematical universe that Chaos mathematics is exploring. A recent film, "The Man Who Knew Infinity," was a true story of a poor Indian man who had no formal education in mathematics, who formulated theorems that were far beyond the known mathematics of his time, and are still at the cutting edge of mathematics theory a century after his time. When the mathematics department at Cambridge University in the UK brought him to their university to study his new theorems, they could not comprehend how a man with no classical mathematics training could understand the highest levels of mathematics beyond what the world could comprehend.

He told them that his theorems came to him in his "meditations" – drifting into his mind from the ether of consciousness. There is a deep pattern to the universe that goes beyond what science can explain at any given moment. Even as Chaos mathematics is beginning to explore deep patterns unfolding within nature, and Taoism was an *ancient* attempt to comprehend these patterns by exploring the universe within. A universe which could only be reached by letting go, a state only achievable in meditative states.

And science is not the only thing that is evolving, as science dispels misunderstandings and misconceptions about Internal Arts and mind-body practices. Religion is also evolving in its attitudes, realizing as the science expands, that Eastern mind-body practices like Tai Chi and Qigong Meditation are not competing with their faith. And in fact can be a supportive part of their spiritual journey. Pope Francis recently made religious history when he recognized Father Thomas Merton in his historic televised speech to the United States Congress.

Father Merton was famous in Catholic circles for being a student and advocate of Eastern mind-body meditative practices, who saw no conflict with them and his religious faith, at a time when much of the church did. Today his vision is honored by the head of his church. At one time the church frowned on the idea of the Earth rotating around the sun, and persecuted people for suggesting that was true. Then science showed it was, and religion evolved to catch up. This is what has happened with Eastern mind-body practices like Tai Chi and Qigong. Eventually it will happen with Taoism as well. As science catches up with them, so will religion.

My life of having a foot in the science of Taoist thought, and another foot in the actual experience of it via Tai Chi and the Internal Arts experience, has opened me to some unique insights which I think can be valuable to all Taoists and Tai Chi teachers and practitioners. At least it can be for those who approach these arts/sciences with the same open mindedness I have. Which is why I opened with a chapter clarifying that Taoism is not a religion, and in no way conflicts or competes with your religious journey. But as Father Merton found, may augment it by clarifying the brain and nervous system. Just as a clearer mind and calmer nervous system can help you hit a baseball better, or take a math test better, that same clarity of thinking could really do nothing but augment one's spiritual or religious journey. Again, there is no Deity in Taoism, because Taoism is an internal mind-body science of discovery of the nature of the universe, and is NOT a religion.

So now that we have moved past that issue, I will now share in the unfolding pages of this book things I could never have learned from books or words. Experiences and insights that are really so huge they are beyond what words can convey. But I will do my best to do so.

These insights have enabled me to see a depth to Tai Chi and Taoism that is very profound. For example, few modern Taoists or Tai Chi enthusiasts, or for that matter few Chaos mathematicians, are probably aware of the fact that the very first example of fractal art and self-replicating theory (pioneered by modern Chaos mathematicians) was found in the ancient Yin Yang symbol, otherwise known as the Tai Chi symbol. This was perhaps the world's first image of fractal art. I will go into more detail of this in the following chapters. But for now it is worth noting that ancient Taoists saw the self-replicating nature of patterns of reality, and created the Yin Yang symbol to represent this deep reality of this mathematical reality. A reality that only in our lifetime Chaos mathematics, with the aid of computer technology, is now able to only begin to explore. I invite you into this new world of East/West, Yin Yang, science/mysticism that is emerging all around us. But in order to do this requires us to diffuse any last remaining superstitious remnants of misunderstanding, about Taoism being a religion that conflicts in any way with religion. It does not, any more than physics and mathematics do. Facts and sciences are not heretical to religion, they are simply facts and sciences, and that is what Taoism is about.

Merriam-Webster dictionary defines religion as, "the belief in a god or in a group of gods." I was first exposed to the Tao te Ching in a world religions class at the university, where I was told that Taoism was a religion. But after 40 years of studying the Tao te Ching, and of having actually "felt" the tactile experience of the Tao, and the energetic nature of myself and the universe, I came to realize that Taoism is not a religion at all. Taoism is rather a verbal description of something that cannot be comprehended in a left-brain, analytical, verbal way —*unless* you have the internal experience of the Tao, the way of the universe, the energy that expands through us, through all things. I have found that Tai Chi and Qigong can be a vehicle to *help* provide that. Tai Chi and the Internal Arts are a new scientific method enabling us to go within, and feel the things that modern biologists and medical scientists are proving with scientific method. Taoism is an ancient scientific method enabling us to explore the reality of Chaos mathematics and physics in a personal, tangible, visceral way.

New cutting edge science is beginning to comprehend more and more about the right brain meditative experience, and its vast potential to enrich our lives and the human condition. Tai Chi is an art designed to take us into this nebulous undefinable experience, and Taoist philosophy offers road signs to help us navigate the inconceivable nature of undefinable experience.

I have found the Tao te Ching integral in my Tai Chi journey for two reasons. It offered verbal concepts that were larger than could be understood. It gives the mind moments that leave the mind open to something larger from those unhinged moments, such as are produced by Zen koans with no answer like, "What is the sound of one hand clapping?" Secondly, the Tao te Ching became a place I could go to after having internal experiences in Tai Chi and Qigong Meditation. Experiences that had no tangible explanation, that were bigger than I could contextualize or comprehend with my brain, or at least with the part of the brain we normally think with. The Tao te Ching provided comfort because when reading Lao Tzu's poetry, those intangible, larger-than-conceivable experiences (that left me feeling so adrift and out of sorts) were somehow described in the nebulous undefined lines of Lao Tzu's poems. And for brief moments my left-brain analytical mind, and my right-brain out of the box mind, would find common ground in those "A-HA!" moments. I would find comfort in knowing that I was not alone – at least Lao Tzu was with me.

When our Tai Chi journey and Taoist journey become inextricably entwined, both are profoundly enhanced by that interweaving.

I found the journey exciting and mind expanding. I think you will too. I have had experiences that if anyone had told me about before I had them, I would have thought them too fantastic to believe.

They have enabled this little exercise called Tai Chi to unfold through me and my practice, in ways that not only changed my life and had a huge impact on me personally, but has connected me with people all over the planet, whose lives were changed by Tai Chi. Together, we created a global Tai Chi movement that has educated millions worldwide about this ancient practice, that is today also a new emerging science known as Tai Chi.

Paradoxically, as we play at these *ancient* forms of Tai Chi, and ponder ancient Taoist philosophy, we often find ourselves now at the *cutting edge* of modern science; as physics and mathematics reach to explain and understand the deeper more subtle patterns of reality, and as medical science's technological advances unveil ever more profound effects of the Internal Arts.

As many Tai Chi devotees pine for the "good old days" of the Internal Arts, I feel that we are living in the MOST exciting times for these Internal Arts. As the Yang modern external technological and the Yin internal world's come together and join hands in a mutual awakening and expansion. The Yin Yang symbol of balance represents this balance of the internal and external worlds, which our generation is at the heart of discovering in more and more profound ways.

In the West and in modern scientific method we look at reality from the outside in, while the ancient mind-body arts of Internal Arts and Taoist philosophy/science explore the same reality from the inside out.

They do not conflict, they do not compete, they are brother and sister of the same exploration of the same reality. Just from different vantage points. And when we see things from different angles we see more than just a one dimensional or two dimensional reality. We can lift up to larger three dimensional perspectives, and see things in their totality with clearer understandings of reality, which we are a part of, just as much as molecules and sub atomic particles under electron microscopes are.

From a Tai Chi and Taoist perspective "we" are the laboratory of discovery. It is an exciting and thrilling journey of discovery, and there is nothing to be afraid of here. Only the joy of pure discovery lies before us. This was the path of Michelangelo who explored reality from both the external Yang study and from the internal Yin study of internal meditative self-exploration techniques, both represented in his most famous work of art on the ceiling of the Sistine Chapel.

The open road is before us. This is a time of high science as ancient mind-body Internal Arts are being validated by science's expanding technological ability to understand our mind, body, and the natural world beneath the surface of manifest reality.

If there was *one* most fascinating time in history to be involved in the

Internal Arts, it would not be "the good old days." It would be the time we are living in now, as science and what have long been considered "mystical" practices are coming together. It is a time of enlightenment. A new renaissance.

It is changing medical science in huge ways that will in time save society vast amounts of healthcare dollars, and will have profoundly positive impacts on society at all levels, education, business, and more. Many of the world's largest corporations are now using Tai Chi, Qigong and Internal Arts to improve productivity and increase profits. More educational institutions are beginning to explore how Internal Arts can improve the educational process and student's ability to absorb and retain information.

As Lao Tzu wrote, by letting go of what we are, we can evolve into what we will become. Tai Chi is perhaps the world's most effective model for learning the art of letting go.

The Taoist Yin Yang – The Tai Chi Symbol

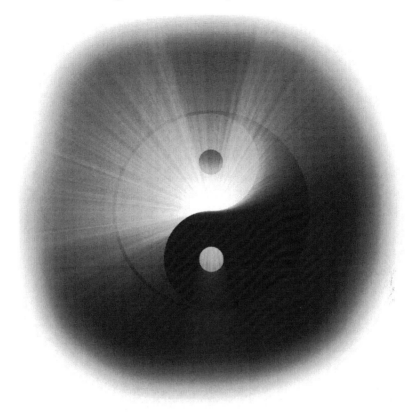

"In a very real sense one can consider **Tai Chi** Chuan
to be a physical expression and manifestation of the
principles and philosophy of **Taoism**."
--Taoism and the Philosophy of Tai Chi Chuan
* Source: www.chebucto.ns.ca/Philosophy/**Taichi/taoism**.html

My Tai Chi teacher, Jais Booth, used to tell us, "First you learn your Tai Chi form, and THEN you can start to learn Tai Chi." One could also say, "First you learn Tai Chi, and then you begin to understand the tides of the universe, the Tao." Taoism is the study and philosophy of the interacting polarities of Yin and Yang, the tides that power the universe. They flow through each of us, just as they flow through the universe, like ocean currents and the ocean winds. Most of humanity is unwittingly washed and dashed upon those currents and waves, with no idea of these unseen forces of nature. Tai Chi as meditation can help us navigate those currents.

Tai Chi is the deepest and most affecting way to become familiar with the flowing tides of Yin and Yang energy, behind, beneath, and within all things in the universe, including us. The human world around us operates, or rather thinks, almost exclusively in a Yang manner: Control, construction, analysis, verbal, rules. Many think that this is the whole world. But it is not, not by a long shot. Taoism teaches us this world, this manifest reality, is only the tiny visible tip of the waves emerging from a deep and limitless ocean of un-manifest, unformed reality, a field of energy from which all things spring from. Perhaps what physicists refer to as the "quantum field," the limitless field of un-manifest *potential* energy from which all particles making up the manifest universe emerge. Others have described this manifest world – the world most consider to be all there is to existence – is akin to the projections of a movie projector on a screen, while the unseen un-manifest nature of reality is the film and projector. The source of this projected reality we think of as the world. Tai Chi, the Internal Arts, and Taoism are scientific methods that can take us beyond the projection and into the projector. Into the film, the directing, the acting, and to the screenplay that lays the groundwork for what we see on the screen. Taoists would say that dealing with the challenges in the world, by only addressing what is manifest, would be as comical and futile as trying to change the course of a film by standing before the projector screen with a magic marker and an eraser. This isn't to say that our physical actions in the world do not matter, but it is simply stating the obvious that there are deeper ways as well.

A simple real world example would be to address high blood pressure only with a drug therapy. This is like standing at the screen of flashing images trying to change the course of the film projected on it. Whereas, by going within via the Internal Arts, we can begin to untangle the thought patterns that cause our minds and hearts to tighten. Which creates physical tension and anxiety, which causes the circulatory system to tighten, which causes the heart to push the blood harder through the system, which results in the damage of chronic hypertension.

The Internal Arts practitioner leaves the screen and the stage, and travels in past the projector light. Past the film, and past the director and actors and into the creative process of the screen writer of this play of our life. Isn't this fascinating? It has taken me a very long time to piece this all together and to comprehend all of this. I hope you enjoy this journey we are taking together in this book, as much as I have enjoyed bringing the fruits of this long amazing journey to its pages. These realizations are not mine alone, they are the fruits of countless lives and journey's throughout the history of humanity. My role was to open to their wisdom, and now to share what I have opened to over the decades. This journey will amaze you, starting here with a huge insight I had about ancient Chinese wisdom while studying acupuncture, which is based on the same concept of our and the universe's energy nature, just as Tai Chi and Taoism are.

Author's note and caveat: To those who would scoff at the idea that Taoism and Quantum Physics have anything to do with one another, I would suggest spending 40 years practicing the Internal Arts and "feeling" the sensations of your internal energetic nature, and to spend a few decades studying the Chinese sciences of the mind and body. But, if you did so and were still unmoved by that, you might still laugh at the concept. Lao Tzu told us that when you speak of the Tao some will laugh. He wrote, if they didn't laugh it would not be the Tao. These concepts stretch the mind so far, that for many they simply retract, closing their minds and dismiss, rather than breathing and opening. I urge you, dear reader, to breathe and open. For it is the way of the Tao, the way of Tai Chi. And it is far more exciting than squeezing the mind closed. Einstein said that "He who can no longer pause to wonder and stand rapt in awe, is as good as dead; his eyes are closed."

Long ago, I studied acupuncture for a year through Japan's Waseda Acupuncture College's United States' program, and it was a mind-blowing experience on many levels. We learned many of the 361 main acupuncture points on the body, and how to locate all of them. As the program progressed, we were exposed to electronic tools that could be used in your acupuncture practice, devices to help you specifically locate acupuncture points on the skin, once you had found the general location in the reference books we were given. The device was not unlike an ohm meter, which could detect the points of "least electrical resistance on the skin." This was because many of the *acupuncture points are located on the points of least electrical resistance on the skin*. Ask yourself this, "How did humans 2,000 years ago, or maybe even 4,000 years ago according to some historians, know where the points of least electrical resistance on the skin were?" Learning this makes one *pause to wonder*. After having done Tai Chi and Qigong for 40 years, I suggest that they may have *attuned* to their internal sensations, and that led them to "feel" where the points were.

In my introductory classes I teach students Sitting Qigong, or Nei Gong energy work meditations. At the end of the session after clearing – or more accurately allowing the energy channels of the mind, heart and body to unload what they squeeze, while still sitting with our eyes closed, I have the students hold their hands about 3 to 4 feet apart, palm facing palm, as if they are holding a large beach ball. Then with eyes still closed, I instruct students "Slowly move your hands in toward one another, opening to the sensation of the energy we've gathered within throughout and all around ourselves, including between our hands, until your hands are almost touching." We do this 3 times, and afterwards slowly open our eyes and discuss the experience. In each new class many people report sensations on their hands: heat, energy, pressure, tingling, or other sensations. Other students often will nod in recognition of what they are describing, obviously having felt it themselves. They are (many for the first time in their lives) sensing their Qi, or life energy. Our first sensation of the energetic tides and winds of the Tao, the way of the universe. When I first experienced this energetic nature of my being, my first thought was, "WOW! Why didn't anyone ever tell me about this?" Followed quickly by this excited thought, "Gee, I wonder what else I can do with this."

Tai Chi is an Internal Art. It can teach us how to access the inner more subtle realms of the un-manifest unformed world of flowing energetic potential from which all existence emerges from. This will all make sense as you read on through this book. Your Tai Chi forms are the Yang manifest, the tip of the wave. But the smoothness, the effortlessness, the power of your Tai Chi forms comes from a deeper more nebulous place that no words can describe. They emerge from the Tao, the unseen, the Yin, the formless. Tai Chi will never intellectually explain these forces, but will enable us to relax out of the way of them, and ride them like a surfer as they flow through us, and through our lives.

When we first begin Tai Chi most of us suffer from a delusion that we will learn some *mental trick*, or figure out some special analytical technique we can "hold in our mind", that will make our Tai Chi good, smooth, and powerful. But, when you do Tai Chi your whole life and look back, you realize that it was this constant immersion in this deeper state of being, this yielding state, this Yin state, that washed away your hard tight edges, and allowed the liquid effortless power of the Yin, the Tao, to flow through your forms like an angel's caress. Nurturing you and massaging you even as you become more powerful. You realize that Tai Chi was never difficult, it was the tight rigid illusions we held in our mind, heart, and body that made us think it was difficult. Tai Chi was really mostly about "letting go," yielding," and becoming Yin.

When we pull, or push, in Tai Chi it is the Dan Tien, our "center of gravity" from where all the pushes or pulls come from. At first it feels like "making it" come from the Dan Tien, but over time, the Dan Tien takes on a mind of its own, and we "surrender" around it, allowing the power of the Dan Tien to flow the movements through our relaxed body ...

This practice of "moving from center" and surrendering to its flow ... can be a model for "surrendering to the flow of the Tao" ... the way of the universe ... the energetic tides washing us to where we are flowing to ...

When we begin to learn Tai Chi the focus is Yang: where to put the foot, the hand, how to hold the body, the head and posture. Then, over time, after we memorize our forms and practice them for the several hundredth, or several thousandth time, our Yang control mind lets go. In that moment we are swept away by the flow of the movements as they move us, and we relax out of the way, to "feel" the tide washing through us. This is the Yin consciousness.

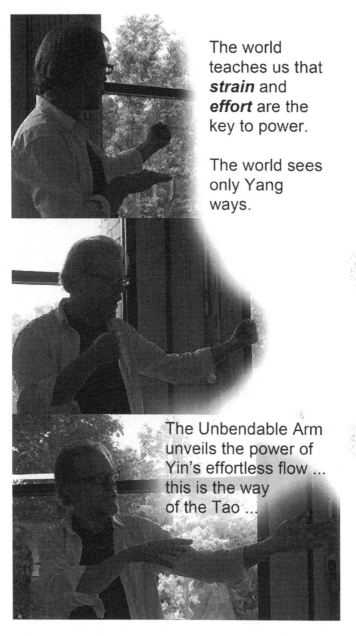

The world teaches us that *strain* and *effort* are the key to power.

The world sees only Yang ways.

The Unbendable Arm unveils the power of Yin's effortless flow ... this is the way of the Tao ...

Single Whip is perhaps the most common Tai Chi movement among all the Tai Chi styles. When we first learn Single Whip our mind is Yang. We memorize how to shape our hand to form a Duck's Beak, how to turn our dan tien [an energy point about 3 thumb widths below our belly button, and 2 thumb widths inside of us], thinking about our body moving with the flow of the arm and hand, where to place our foot, and how to shift from one leg to another. Then, over time, the movements of hands and feet begin to become part of the flow moving through us, as the dan tien moves us effortlessly as the flow moves through us.

As the dan tien moves us effortlessly we sink and surrender to its motion, and everything else follows in line with the flowing swirling dan tien. We no longer "control" the movement. We "yield" to the movement flowing through us. Our Tai Chi transforms from Yang to Yin over the months and years.

When we look back over decades of Tai Chi practice ...

we see that we once thought we had to "hold" our postures ...

unti we realize that we now find ourselves freefalling into them ...

and that is when all doors open ...

When our Tai Chi is Yin, our main awareness is not of how we are "performing" the movements, but of how much we are surrendering, "sinking" as the movements flow us. We surrender everything we are to gravity as we sink into postures, and we surrender out of the way of the flow of the Single Whip and all the postures. In that moment, the Tao, the universal energy, has space to flow through us. That is when we feel an effortless power that is greater than anything we could ever control in our muscles, or hold in our mind.

My first book, "The Complete Idiot's Guide to T'ai Chi & Qigong" just came out in 4th edition through Bantam-Penguin, In this new 4th edition I put an exercise called "The Unbendable Arm" right at the front of the book, because I wanted those who had no experience in the concept of Yin power, or effortless power, to get a sense of it. It blows people's minds when they are exposed to it.

Why does it blow their mind? It opens a whole new paradigm of viewing the world and their place in it. They have been taught their entire life that important things are actions involving force and strain and effort. To realize that great power comes from "letting go" shakes the foundations of their view of the world and themselves. This is the power of the Yin being exemplified in the Unbendable Arm.

For those unfamiliar with the Unbendable Arm, it is an exercise where students try to hold their arms out straight, while a partner student tries to bend it at the elbow. Usually the partner can bend it, even as the student strains their muscles to resist.

Then the student with the extended arm is instructed to close their eyes, and open to a downpour of energy flowing down through their body, through their feet, and down into the earth. And to also let the energy flow through their shoulder, arm, and out through their hand and fingers. Flowing on out through the wall and through all the walls in that part of the city and beyond.

When the student feels a sense of their shoulder and arm being like a hollow tube of bamboo with the breeze blowing through it, they give their partner a nod, and the partner again tries to bend the arm. They can't. Not only can they not bend it, but the partner's Unbendable Arm is relaxed. The muscles are not tight and straining beneath their pushing hands, as they try to bend the arm.

In image #1 (above) I resist with muscles, and in image #2 the more powerful student is able to bend my arm. In image #3 (bottom), I relax, envisioning the flow of Qi, and my relaxed arm is unbendable. No matter how hard the student tries, he cannot bend it.

Many students can do this the very first time. Some require a bit more coaching. But almost without exception every new student in the class is able to do this. For those that struggle with it, they are almost always trying too hard to "make something happen," rather than relaxing out of the way of the sense of flow pouring through them.

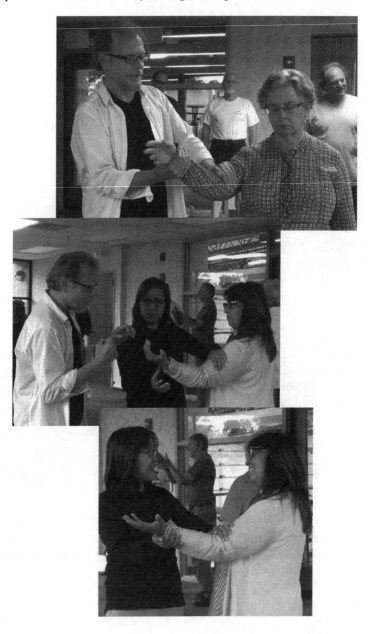

This is the power of Yin. This is the essence of Tai Chi. Once we learn the forms, then our lives are spent learning how to "let go" around the forms, to allow the forms to "flow through" us. In this way, we are training ourselves to open to effortless Yin power in every action of our lives.

Swimming provides the most use of the body of all standard exercises. If you do several strokes of swimming you can rotate the body in about 65% of the ways it can move. Tai Chi, however, is the ultimate way to do this. A Tai Chi long form rotates the body in about 95% of the ways it can move. So this practice of relaxing out of the way of our moves, and allowing them to "flow through us," just as we allow the energy to flow through our Unbendable Arm, translates into a life of Yin, of effortless power. All of our physical actions in our life can open to this.

To clarify, if you've been in any Tai Chi discussion boards on the internet, some Tai Chi enthusiasts challenge the usefulness of the "unbendable arm" exercise. This is because they do not believe that the Qi or energy flowing through the arm is real. This challenge actually helps make the point I am trying to make here.

It does not matter if the Qi itself is real or not in this case, because the *imagery* of *sensing* that feeling of effortless flow through the arm triggers the deepest skeletal muscles to go into action. It allows the gross muscles of the arm to relax. This results in a very effortless unbendable arm. You cannot "will" these deep skeletal muscles into action using the Yang analytical control mind. It can only happen when you surrender to the Yin sensation of flow. Those who get caught up in this *argument* are Yang/control focused in their Tai Chi, just as most of the world is.

This shift in our lives from Yang control to Yin surrender/sensation changes everything, physically, mentally and emotionally. Essentially in every way imaginable, and even beyond what can be imagined. We become more graceful, more yielding, easier to get along with, more deeply expressive with less sharp edges, and most of all we become more nurturing.

In the Yin Yang, the Tai Chi symbol, the Yin/dark half of the waves is the feminine. The white half is the Yang, the masculine. The world operates in Yang masculine ways for the most part. But it is nurtured by the Yin. Our finding balance in the Internal Arts, the Yin arts, will nurture us and it will nurture those around us. As these arts spread around the world, it will nurture all of humanity and our planet.

Lao Tzu said the universal energy, the Tao, nurtures all things. When you learn your forms well enough to relax out of the way of them, and let that Yin effortless force flow through you, you have become part of a priesthood of sorts. Not of a religion, but rather part of a brotherhood and sisterhood, of people who have experienced a larger reality. When we "let go" of the myth of our individuality, and let go of our grip on what we think the world is, we see ourselves more as connected to everything. Part of a field of life, a life-force or life energy, a field of Qi.

Whether it is actual or the result of mental imagery does not matter, because the effect this shift has in our lives is real, regardless.

By joining the ancient and global family of this deeper form of Tai Chi, you have become a nurturing force in this planet, a Yin force that nurtures all things. You have become *more real*.

"A human being is a part of a whole, called by us a universe, a part limited in time and space. He experiences himself, his thoughts and feelings as something separated from the rest . . . a kind of optical delusion of his consciousness. This delusion is a kind of prison for us, restricting us to our personal desires and to affection for a few persons nearest to us. Our task must be to free ourselves from this prison by widening our circle of compassion to embrace all living creatures and the whole of nature in its beauty."
-- Albert Einstein

The Physics of the Tao, of Tai Chi, of You

Years ago, I attended a world conference of the Institute of Noetic Sciences, an organization founded by astronaut Edgar Mitchell. The institute was created to study and better understand the human mind and its connection with, and effect on, the world around us. If you have not yet attended their annual conference, I highly recommend it.

I was walking through the conference, which was located in the gorgeous mountain city of Boulder, Colorado, United States, not intending to stay for the current speaker. Then something she said stopped me in my tracks. The speaker was a physicist by trade. But she was also a meditation teacher in her spare time. As I moved toward the exit door, I heard her introduce herself and say "When we experience mind-body meditative practices, we often feel 'lighter' when we are done. We tell ourselves that this is a hypnotic delusion we created in our minds, but actually, as a physicist, I can tell you that this is actually when we feel the most real."

As most people who practice Qigong meditation and Tai Chi as an energy or Qi meditation, I had experienced that sense of "lightness of being" after practicing my Internal Arts. I suddenly forgot about where I was going in such a hurry, and became riveted as this physicist explained exactly why that sensation we feel is when we are feeling the *most real*.

This physicist explained our true nature as beings in this universe, by describing the makeup of atoms. It was an explanation of atoms I would hear repeated decades later when Neil deGrasse Tyson, (American astrophysicist, cosmologist, author, and Frederick P. Rose Director of the Hayden Planetarium at the Rose Center for Earth and Space in New York City) recreated an updated version of Carl Sagan's world renowned science series, "Cosmos," in which Dr. Tyson described the almost unbelievably spacious subatomic nature of our being.

But it had been the woman physicist and meditation teacher in Boulder, Colorado who first blew my mind with this description of that atom. Her description of the atoms that make up me and you explained exactly why meditation made me feel "lighter," and why that lighter feeling was more real than the illusion of the denser perception of ourselves, which most people walk around holding in their minds.

She told a transfixed crowd of people from around the world that if you could take an atom out of anything in the universe, such as out of your own body, and somehow blow it up to make it large enough to see with the naked eye, it would be the size of an American football field. The nucleus of the atom would be the size of a BB on the 50 yard line, while the electrons going around it would be the size of dust motes 50 yards away in the end zone. Everything between the BB and the dust mote 50 yards away would be "empty space, or potential energy field."

This was nothing like what I had been raised to think atoms looked like. I remembered the atom models in science class in high school, with the large blue ball in the center, with slightly smaller orange balls around it, connected by tinker-toy type sticks. That image left us with the idea that the universe was made out of the clunky balls with little space between them, and no mention of the vast energy field we are made of.

The physicist further blew our minds on that beautiful Colorado day high in the Rocky Mountains, when she took this image a step further, so we could see how truly spacious we are. She said that if you could somehow get rid of all that empty space, or potential energy field we are made of, and somehow smush all the sub-atomic particles together ... the entire human race ... the entirety of humanity, would only add up to one single grain of rice. WOW!

Since that day, I have told this story to thousands of new Tai Chi students in my classes, the last moment before we close our eyes, and I take them into their first Sitting Qigong, or Nei Gong, energy meditation. I tell them at this moment, because it leaves them feeling as if the wind could blow right through them. And that is a perfect mood setting to open to the experience of energy work meditation, to being open to the tides and winds of the Qi, or life energy, that flows through us all the time.

It is no longer Chinese mystics who are telling us that we are energy beings. It is quantum physicists. The world has come full circle.

Another scientific experience really brought this reality of the open and spacious nature of our being home to me. When I first began learning Nei Gong meditations in my Tai Chi training, my children were young and we often took them to the famed Griffith Park Observatory in Los Angeles, California (USA). This observatory has been pictured in several movies, including James Dean's "Rebel Without a Cause." In that observatory was a Particle Chamber made of glass, which had bright lights inside and was filled with an ammonia mist. It was designed to make cosmic particles falling down through space observable to the naked eye. The ammonia mist wrapped layers of itself around the falling cosmic particles, and the flood lights in the chamber illuminated them to make them clearly visible. It was like a blizzard of white particles falling through space, through that chamber, as the observatory guide explained to us that these cosmic particles were falling through the concrete roof of the observatory, down through our skulls and brains and bodies, through our tennis shoes, and on down into the earth.

My curiosity was peeked because of my Nei Gong training, which invoked images of Qi or energy flowing through my body. This had tested me at first, because I suffered from the illusion that our heads, skulls and body were a solid impenetrable mass. This tightened my head with resistance, not conscious, but *subliminal* resistance. So, I reached out my arm over the Particle Chamber to see if my "solid" body would block the downpour of cosmic particles pouring through the particle chamber beneath my arm in any way. It didn't. The blizzard of particles beneath my arm was just as thick as it was all around my arm. It was as if I was not even physical. I was spacious and porous and open, and this experience freed my mind to the idea that Qi could flow through me just as easily.

So today I also share this experience with students, to help them let go of the illusion that they are solid mass, and that subtle energies can't flow through them. Because if they suffer from that delusion, they unconsciously tighten their heads when I invoke the image of Qi or light pouring through or expanding through their skulls and bodies. This interferes with their ability to enjoy Nei Gong, and ultimately Tai Chi in the deepest way. Knowing we are open and spacious energetic beings facilitates the Qi imagery of Tai Chi's depth and benefit to students. If you teach, feel free to share my physics experiences with your students as I do with my own. It is a great teaching tool. I also recommend the Tao te Ching to all my students.

Lao Tzu's Tao te Ching can help our minds un-grip from what Einstein called "the delusion," that we are separate from the rest of the universe, because just as Einstein said, that is a delusion. Tai Chi and Qigong can enable us to let go deeper and deeper over the months and years of our practice. To feel the flow, the effortlessness, the openness of our being that is waiting to shine through us, as we let our Internal Arts untangle us. We do not "make" our tangles go away, it is not an act of will. It is a "letting," not a "making."

We begin to feel the reality of what we are, energy beings who can tighten our being with gripping thoughts. Or we can breathe, open and yield to the tides and winds of energy, the field, the Tao waiting to flow through us when we loosen and let go. And when this happens we feel not only lighter, but larger. This is not a delusion, for we are expansive beings of light or energy, limitless in nature.

This is the highest purpose of Tai Chi, to untangle the mind, heart, and body, so that we can open to the flow of energy waiting to wash, or expand, through us. We begin with the Yang structural building of our Tai Chi forms, and then spend our lives trying to *relax out of the way* of them. Or as Bruce Lee wrote, we learn our forms and then try to forget everything we learned, so that a raw spontaneity can flow through us. Lao Tzu put it in other words, urging us to know the masculine, the Yang, but to keep to the feminine, the Yin, the wellspring from where all things flow from.

This is not a religion, but there is a great spirituality to it. Because to truly open to and flow with the energy waiting to course through us, we have to "let go." Let go of who we are, what we desire, our pride, our angers, our grudges, our prejudice, and our hatred. It is the way of Tai Chi. It is the way of the Tao.

When we let go and open to this state of flow, we drift on the winds and tides of the energy flowing through us, carrying us through our forms. And ultimately through our lives. It is also the moment when we let go of a "sense of self," and we feel "connected to everything," part of the field of *all* existence.

It is interesting that neurological research in plasticity, the study of how the human brain and nervous system are actually changing and evolving (or devolving, depending on our habits and thoughts), led researchers to discover that meditation and also prayer can actually lessen function in the part of the brain that feels "isolation," and increase function in the part of the brain that makes us feel "connected."

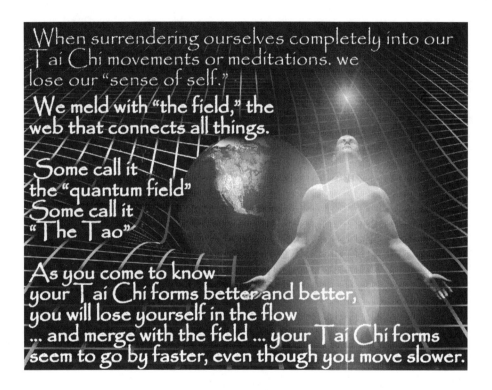

When surrendering ourselves completely into our Tai Chi movements or meditations. we lose our "sense of self."
We meld with "the field," the web that connects all things.
Some call it the "quantum field"
Some call it "The Tao"
As you come to know your Tai Chi forms better and better, you will lose yourself in the flow ... and merge with the field ... your Tai Chi forms seem to go by faster, even though you move slower.

That is the one thing that stuck with me the most, from the first night of my first Tai Chi and Qigong Meditation class so many decades ago. When I walked out of the class into the cool California moonlit night, and looked up through the trees swaying in the ocean breeze to the platinum moon – I felt connected – to *everything*. As a Kansas-bred boy, I had begun to feel so isolated and alone in California's strange urban sprawl, in a land I wasn't familiar with and felt so out of place in at first. But that night, that night I felt "connected," like I belonged here in this place, on this planet. And it wasn't just California. As a good friend of mine once told me, "No matter where you go, there you are." We often spend a great deal of time always trying to get to something, to someplace, where we will feel better about our lives. Internal Arts' meditative practices literally change our brain structure to enable us to realize that we are already there, even as they may be carrying us to even more wondrous moments, achievements and destinations in our lives.

When we first start Tai Chi we have many ideas of what Tai Chi is. For many students I've taught over the decades of teaching, in corporations, hospitals, schools, prisons, etc., not all, but many students think Tai Chi is only about moving your physical arms and legs to become stronger and more powerful. Including myself, when I started my Tai Chi journey.

In fact, in the beginning I would tighten in stances, straining to make them hard, like isometrics, because my upbringing had taught me that there could be no value in anything that wasn't hard. I continued down this path, until one night my teacher, Jais Booth, put her hand on my shoulder and told me, "Bill, this doesn't have to be hard, it is not supposed to be hard, it can be so much easier." I didn't realize it at the time, but she wasn't just talking about my Tai Chi. She was teaching me about my life.

While it is true that Tai Chi makes you stronger and more powerful, that concept of strength and power we have as novice students was only a shadow of what we would see in coming years. We would learn there was something more powerful than we could squeeze in our ego mind, more powerful than we could control, and we would have to let go of our desire for power and control in order to open to this greater thing.

The Tai Chi journey can be purely physical if that is where we want it to stop. It can be purely a relaxation exercise, if that is where we want it to stop. But, even if that is all we think our Tai Chi journey is, often it will surprise us, and we will have moments where something opens. And then *everything shifts*, and in these moments our being and our world tilt and expand and transform into larger things, more effortless and vast than we could ever put into words.

When we relax out of the way, the planet Earth is behind our pushes and punches ...

When we "tighten up" all we have behind a punch is our fragile back

The "Unbendable Arm" illustrates the essence of Tai Chi's Yin nature ...

Lao Tzu said that the Tao that can be spoken of is not the *true Tao* – he was speaking of consciousness in mathematical terms. The fact that a "set cannot contain itself," is something all mathematicians know. The vast experiences of the universe which Internal Arts can open doors to "cannot be contained in words created by the human mind." That would be like trying to contain a mathematical set within itself. Consciousness operates in this way on a mathematical level. A set cannot contain itself because, to be contained, it always requires a larger set, just as to encase a box always requires a larger box. So when we practice Internal Arts and open to Taoism's larger perceptions of life, how could these larger perceptions possibly be contained within the framework of how we see the world right now at this moment?

When I notice some practice or meditation we do is stretching my students, and I see that they are doubtful of whether they are doing it right, or doing anything at all, because it seems so strange and intangible, I remind my students, "It is okay that you don't understand what we are doing right now. You will understand in retrospect, looking back, after practicing these meditative arts over time. You will learn that it is okay to freefall into newer, larger experiences than you can understand at any given moment. As you allow this to happen your consciousness will over time open to larger *sets* and see yourself and these things in new and larger ways."

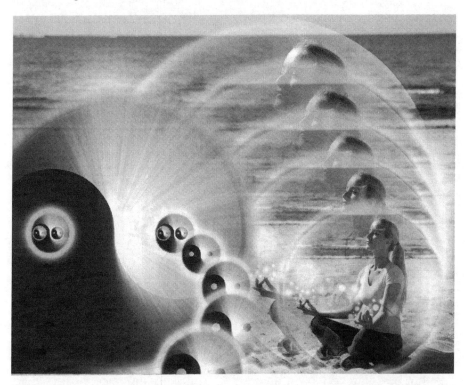

We must free ourselves from the *need* to verbally describe what we experience, in order to expand beyond "the set" of what we know or can describe. Our experience is larger than words. Words are fantastic tools to help us convey experiences we have had to other humans. But our minds are capable of expanding and freefalling, to depths, widths and heights far beyond what has been conceived or will ever be described. My Tai Chi and Qigong journey could never have happened had I felt it necessary to describe all that I was experiencing – the words would have become a prison, limiting my freedom of experience, diminishing my Internal Arts, my Tai Chi and Qigong experience, to only what words could describe.

A huge paradigm for me happened in Tai Chi class one night. In the beginning of my Tai Chi journey, my mind had a habit of constantly trying to analyze and understand and figure out how I could explain the things I was experiencing to others, so that my friends and family wouldn't think I was weird.

One day I realized that I no longer cared if anyone thought I was weird, and I suddenly no longer had any need to describe or articulate what I was experiencing. That moment of liberation enabled me to let go and freefall, and be lifted, drifted, and expanded to places and in ways beyond words, beyond prior experience. It was exquisite.

The Tao that can be told, can never be the true Tao.

Tai Chi--Windows in the Structures of Life

I went to a book signing of a new book by a Harvard architectural-psychologist. Her book told of the new science of how architecture can have a healing impact on our bodies and minds, perhaps not unlike the Chinese architectural design art of Feng Shui. Feng Shui is rooted in Taoism's concept of a universal flow of energy within, throughout, and around all things. Just as many Tai Chi masters see Tai Chi is rooted in Taoism's universal energy, and how we can allow it to flow through our forms and our lives.

She discussed scientific research showing that patients being treated for exactly the same health issues in hospitals healed much faster if their rooms had a view of nature, over patients whose hospital room had a view of a another building's wall.

This architectural-psychologist described how a building's construction is a material Yang concept or action. While the "windows or open spaces" were a Yin-energy concept, that has no material functionality in a centrally heated and air-conditioned home or building. Yet the Yin nonfunctional windows and open spaces do change the consciousness of the room, giving it life, and thereby affecting all the health and actions of the residents who enjoy that light and space. Windows and open space are "Yin."

Tai Chi is known as an "Internal art," a Yin art that in itself would appear to a casual observer to have no tangible functional value. Yet by promoting "space and openness" into our existence, Tai Chi benefits everything we do, whether it be martial arts, sports, any performance, or just enhancing, solidifying, and adding power to all the things we do in our lives. And lets us do them with more grace and less damage to the body.

Yang is walls, construction, and utility. Yin is holes, open spaces, and flow. Our modern world values the Yang quality of things most. We see the Yin as extraneous, even frivolous decorations in life. However, anyone who has had the misfortune of working in a company or factory that has no windows, knows that the lack of Yin open space profoundly affects all aspects of the business. It depresses and causes anxiety in the people who make up that business. Just as anyone who has done Tai Chi at work knows that work goes far better when they, or better yet, their team does their Tai Chi at work.

In the world the Yin is barely noticed, and the Yang is extolled. Lao Tzu, the father of Taoist philosophy, recommended that we 'know the [Yang], the masculine.' But he also warned us to 'keep to the [Yin], the feminine, because the Yin is the mother of all things.' Tai Chi is based upon "yielding" and "receding," not force and conquest. This is the most powerful thing in the universe. Our world needs the balance of Yin, because it is overbalanced in Yang, and Tai Chi can help the world find that balance.

A few days ago I was late for a Tai Chi class, stuck in traffic in a traffic jam. So I breathed and let go of my rush, my grip, my Yang urgency about being late, and sighed and relaxed into a Yin receptive state. I then turned on NPR radio. A historian, discussing the origins of American democracy, made a point I had never heard or considered, but it was a profound point about the power of Yin in our world.

He said the quintessential point in U.S. history ensuring the future of our democracy was not a Yang action, but a Yin yielding. It was the moment that President Washington, our very first President, *stepped down* from the Presidency after his 2nd term, as the rules dictated he should. Most people of that time held their breath, thinking he would never yield power. No one ever had before. His "yielding" gave birth to our democracy.

Some may think of all the other actions that led to U.S. democracy, namely the revolution. It is likely the revolution would have occurred without Washington, because of the national mood. But, only one man could have yielded power he wasn't forced to yield. Washington's personal Yin power profoundly changed history.

Tai Chi helps us cultivate the ability to yield, to let go … the *greatest power*, according to Taoism. Something the world needs, a skill that should be shared as widely as possible.

Yin Yang is the Tai Chi Symbol

"Tai Chi is about letting go of everything that we are, so that we can open to allowing the undefinable evolution of what we are becoming to flow through us. I hope you will read this book in that spirit because I guarantee it will stretch the frontiers of the world you hold in your mind and heart."
-- William Edward Douglas, Jr., author's note

Lao Tzu told us that we have to let go of everything we are, so we can become the thing we will become. I wrote this book because, after nearly 40 years of Tai Chi study, I have found that understanding the Tao, the Way of the Universe, helps take our Tai Chi to vast and profound planes. Diving deep into the world of Taoist philosophy can not only weave into our Tai Chi practice, but can also allow our Tai Chi to weave deeply into our lives as a whole new lifestyle.

We think of the Yin Yang or Tai Chi symbol as "balance" that keeps the world spinning around and around. However, Tai Chi practice can help us "live" this Taoist symbol and the balance it represents. When we do that over the years of our lives, we see that it is not about just going around and around and around. It is about that spinning balance taking on an "upward spiral," lifting and evolving into newness, effervescence, and higher realms of possibility for ourselves and our world.

I was told of a book called "Flatland." The way it was described to me, it was about a one dimensional worm-being whose entire race follows a one dimensional path, a straight line, so that their whole universe is basically only the butt of the one dimensional being in front of them. Then one day, this being got an urge to "turn left" and then turned right, and found an entirely new and expansive two dimensional existence opening up. His friends thought he was "weird." Undaunted, the being eventually even lifted up off the two dimensional plane and an extraordinary "three dimensional" world came into being all around him, being able to look down and see patterns and possibilities unfolding all around and within him. His friends thought him insane when he tried to describe what he'd seen, and laughed at him. Lao Tzu wrote that when you speak of the Tao you will be laughed at by some.

The Yin Yang symbol is at the core of both Taoist thought, and Tai Chi's essence. Understanding the Tao, the Way of the Universe, and its interplay of Yin and Yang, can have a huge impact on our Tai Chi play. But in addition to that it reveals how Tai Chi and the Internal Arts can impact the future of humanity and our world. Taoist philosophy, the Yin Yang, enables us to see how our Tai Chi is a microcosm of the macrocosm of society and our world. Taoism shows us how the same dynamics at play within us, are also at play in society and the world. Lao Tzu told us that when we master ourselves we master the universe. This book shows how this was not just poetic metaphor, but a real life reality. Tai Chi and Qigong offer humanity a way to evolve that will help ensure a future we can all love living in, by helping us to "find our balance." This is what the Yin-Yang Tai Chi symbol represents – balance.

Our modern world today is far over-balanced in the Yang/masculine way, as are our individual lives. The history of humanity has been a constant movement toward this since the dawn of civilization. The modus operandi for humanity has been to explore, conquer, and exploit resources. A very Yang/masculine approach, since our earliest beginnings as a human race.

However, today we are rapidly approaching 8 billion people on the planet. The planet is saturated with people and its resources are being stretched to the limits. Our very existence as a human race and as individuals is demanding of us an evolution toward a more Yin/feminine way. What does that mean? Here's a vivid image to help bring it home. If a masculine Yang force went into a kitchen's larder, its behavior would dictate 'sticking a flag in that larder and claiming it as its own.' While a feminine Yin approach would be to 'survey the larder and try to determine how to best use its contents to nurture and nourish the entire household.' In this case the population of planet Earth.

Western health practices, surgery and pharmaceuticals are very Yang. They *attack* the problems they take on. Chinese Traditional Medicine, which Tai Chi and Qigong are a part of, are designed to nourish and nurture the parts of our body or being that lack Qi, or life energy. Rather than attacking individual things, the goal is to nurture the whole system of life, our bodies or our planet. When we practice Tai Chi it boosts our immune system, improves our breathing, treats heart problems and heart disease, reduces allergy problems, reduces depression and anxiety, etc. This saves society hundreds of thousands of dollars per person in future health costs, and trillions when multiplied by the billions of people on the planet. This further reduces stress planet-wide, and creates a calmer more harmonious planet. This is the Yin way, the feminine way. Tai Chi and Qigong are known as the "Internal Arts," the Yin arts.

Again, Lao Tzu, the father of Taoist philosophy, extolled us to "know the masculine," but then warned us to "keep to the feminine." This is the essence of Tai Chi learning and performing. The Yin Yang symbol, also known as the Tai Chi symbol, contains the white wave with the black dot, representing the Yang masculine aspect of the universe, while the black wave with the white dot represents the Yin feminine aspect of the universe. All things in the universe are made of the interplay of Yin and Yang energy. Society and societal actions can have Yin and Yang qualities, personal conduct, personal actions. The natural world can be described in this way as well.

Learning Tai Chi movements is done in Yang or masculine consciousness, a left-brain analytical action of *control* – learning what the moves are, how to perform them, where to place feet and hands, posture, alignment, and breathing techniques. Then, as one practices these aspects of the forms again and again, the cellular memory becomes so strong that the movements begin to "move you, as you relax out of the way." In this Yin or feminine state, there is no control, there is only yielding to the larger forces rooting you into the earth. Expanding up and out through your forms, pouring through you like a powerful current that is the opposite of effort, more graceful and more potent than one could ever be on their own.

As I mentioned before, it is worth noting that Bruce Lee wrote that true power is found in absolute relaxation. We learn all we can about our forms, and then try to forget all that we have learned so that a formless force of spontaneity can surge through us. His insight captures the essence of Tai Chi and Taoist philosophy.

It has taken me nearly 60 years to come to terms with what I am sharing in this book. One day I realized that I will not be here forever, and felt it would be a shame not to share what I have witnessed unfolding through over 5 decades of Qigong, Tai Chi, and Taoist study.

What if our world is taking the same course as the microcosm of our Tai Chi learning does? What if, as in Tai Chi training, humanity has come this far, learning all the moves in a Yang approach, and is now ready to flow in a more effortless Yin approach?

Can the Internal Arts of Tai Chi and Qigong help usher in a more elegant and effortless future for humanity? Given the profound medical benefits scientific research is proving they offer society, we may not be far from these arts being taught in public schools worldwide. What impact will an entire planet of children and students learning and practicing the internal Yin arts have on our future?

My Taoist Yin-Yang Tai Chi Story

Many years ago, I attended a presentation by Ken Cohen, the master who wrote the legendary book "The Way of Qigong: The Science of Chinese Energy Healing." During his talk, he told us a slide of his Chinese Qigong master. Then an image of an ancient Chinese face appeared on the large screen, one that looked like it had seen a thousand miles and a thousand years, with lines that told stories that words could never tell. Yet the most prominent feature looking down at us was this huge face splitting grin. A kind of mischievous one that made you unable to resist smiling too, as you beheld that face. Master Cohen told us that he had once asked his master, "I've heard it said that Qigong can develop character in a practitioner, is that true?" Ken said his master had replied with that smile, saying, "I do not know about that, but, Qigong will definitely make you into a character."

We had all laughed at that, and perhaps because it tickled my funny bone it stuck in my mind forever. Over time I realized that it wasn't just a funny story, but it was an extremely profound insight into Qigong and its little sister, Tai Chi, and the Taoist way that these Internal/Yin Arts can cultivate.

It has taken me over 5 decades of experience in the Internal Arts before I could screw up the courage to write this book on the Tao of Tai Chi. Why? Because I knew that some would laugh at it. However, Lao Tzu told us that 'if it were not laughed at, it would not be the true Tao.'

When I began Tai Chi study formally, about 40 years ago, my largest struggle was with all of this Internal experience. It was so new, so different than anything I had experienced before. I had this fear in my mind that my friends and family would think I was odd or strange. So my mind was constantly trying to "make sense" of my experiences, trying to analyze, to understand, to articulate and describe every experience I was having. This was a prison for my experience, keeping it caged within an old Yang way of experiencing myself and my world.

Lao Tzu told us that 'the Tao that could be articulated in words, was not the true Tao.' The other day, after over 40 years of formal study of the

...rts, I had an epiphany while teaching a Tai Chi class. I ...d that my true Tai Chi experience had begun when I no longer ...d whether I could explain to anyone what I was experiencing in my ...ai Chi and Qigong Internal adventure. When I no longer cared if my friends or family thought I was strange or crazy, and I no longer had to make sense of what I was experiencing, and I no longer had to "understand" what was happening to me – I was liberated.

I looked back and realized that that had been *the moment* when I had truly begun to "experience the Tao" flowing through me. That was when I had "become a character," in the words of Ken Cohen's ancient master. This epiphany had come during my Tai Chi class, as the beautiful white clouds passed by the large Kansas blue sky out the windows of our studio. It was as I and all the students in the class fell into that state of non-thought, where we merge with the field and feel sublimely connected to everything. A state that, in the humorous words of the greatest U.S. Tai Chi champion David-Dorian Ross, leaves us all with that slack and sublime "Tai Chi poop face." It was in that moment I decided to write this book, and looked forward to some laughing at it, because that would tell me that it had touched the essence of Tai Chi, the essence of the Tao.

Although my formal Tai Chi and Qigong study began about 40 years ago, I actually began studying Qigong almost 15 years prior to that. When you read the following, please do so with an open Tai Chi mind, as I describe an experience that goes far beyond the Yang explainable world. It took me a lifetime to see this in perspective. Without all those decades of allowing Tai Chi and Qigong to loosen me beyond my borders and boundaries, I would have never been able to truly come to terms with these amazing experiences in my life. I understand now, that Tai Chi's constant loosening of my being – physically, emotionally, mentally, and beyond – was a training ground for perceiving a much larger world than my "old set" of consciousness was capable of comprehending.

My first Qigong teacher was not human, it was an angel, or at least that was how my six year old mind saw this ethereal being. A being that had come to me in the middle of the night, to share insights with me that would change my life and my world, in ways that a six year old western Kansas boy could never have dreamed possible.

That simple innocent six year old Kansas boy could never have imagined that less than 15 years later he would meet a girl from the other side of the planet with a similar experience. A girl whose mother had taught her Qigong (breathing lessons) and Tai Chi in her garden. In 1963, when the angel had visited me to give me my very first Qigong (breathing) lesson, on the other side of the planet, a young Chinese girl (that I would one day marry) stood alone in her white confirmation dress. She stood in her mother's garden where she had studied Tai Chi and Qigong with her Mom, and was seeing a vision of Mother Mary floating in her garden watching her. This vision was just as real to her as was her mother and father, who were busy in the house preparing her confirmation day celebration meal. Little Oi Yue (Angela) Wong stood open mouthed in her garden, having an extraordinary ethereal experience.

Nor could the small Kansas boy I was have ever imagined that I would soon begin learning Tai Chi with this young woman. That our study would open my mind to Taoist philosophy, in an attempt to comprehend the vast universes Tai Chi and Qigong were opening in my mind and my life. That small boy I was could have never understood how this Taoist, Tai Chi, and Qigong study and practice over decades, would prepare us to begin teaching Tai Chi and Qigong in schools, prisons, hospitals, corporations, churches, synagogues, and around the world. And would help other teachers worldwide expand their teaching into churches, mosques, synagogues, prisons, hospitals, corporations, schools, and all levels of their communities and societies.

That boy would have thought you were insane if you had told him that he and this girl from the other side of the planet would found an event that would lead them to the farthest corners of the earth. To be the official guest of the Brazilian government, or to dine with officials in Perth Australia's City Council penthouse restaurant, or meet with U.S. Cultural Affairs officials in Hong Kong, or speak with officials in the Hong Kong government. And would later be hosted to speak in Africa: Cameroon and Tunisia, about this global event we had founded – an event which would be officially proclaimed by governors of 22 US

States; many senates, including: California, Puerto Rico, New York; and city councils' from Europe to Latin America to Australia; and by the National Congress of Brazil. This boy would have never been able to comprehend that this event they would form in their minds would spread around the world, and be covered by CNN, the New York Times, BBC Television, Agence France Presse Television, Egyptian national news, Brazilian national news, and on and on. And that the events they reported on would be celebrated all on the same day, in hundreds of cities in over 80 nations each year.

That night in 1963, almost 55 years ago, the angel gave me my first breathing lesson (the same year my wife as a young girl was experiencing a spiritual vision in her mother's Tai Chi garden). That night so long ago, that angel drew me out of my warm bed and held my 6 year old body in its ethereal arms. It flew me to a small alleyway between my parent's Lutheran Church, and the Sunday school I attended in the building next to it. The angel set me down in the small alleyway and proceeded to give me "breathing lessons." About 15 years later, I would learn that Qigong, which came from China, meant "breathing lessons" in Chinese, and I would embark on a journey that would help me discover mind-body tools. Tools that would help me unfold my world, revealing that I had been living in a one dimensional world. But now I could begin to "turn left" and then right, and spiral upward to a three dimensional world far beyond anything my wildest imaginings could have conceived of before.

As the small boy I was followed the angel's "breathing" instructions, I began to lift off the pavement. Little by little, I lifted higher and higher until I was flying in large looping circles, up towards the platinum moon above the church and Sunday school, and then back down to the alleyway between them. At first I would become afraid of this larger reality, and then would tighten and hold my breath, and begin to fall. What I would realize over the coming decades of my life, was that the angel's lesson was not just about breathing. It was about a new way of seeing life and the world. The angel was speaking to the young six year-old boy I was then in "symbols."

In time, over a lifetime of study of the Internal Arts and Taoist philosophy, I began to realize that the Sunday school had represented the *Yang, masculine*, controlled, intellectual, manifest consciousness. The world most people consider all of existence. While the Church had represented the *Yin, feminine*, uncontrolled, nebulous, unformed, energetic-spiritual realms of meditative consciousness. I would later remember this scene when I would read Lao Tzu's words about the importance of 'knowing the masculine,' but 'keeping to the feminine … the wellspring of all things.'

When I would look back over the 60 years of my life and see how a worldwide event that had touched millions in positive ways, had sprung from emptiness, from my mediation, from the Yin consciousness, from Lao Tzu's 'wellspring of all things.' I realized that if I had gripped my life in the Yang, control, masculine way of the world, none of this could have happened. The angel's lessons and all the 50 years of lessons made such clear sense, and perhaps boded something for the world.

I saw that perhaps a new world could become possible if humanity had more access to the Yin consciousness. And that Tai Chi and Qigong were powerful vehicles to shedding off the tangles of tight control and stress, to allow space for the nebulous, unformed possibility to expand through our world. And this at a time when creativity, newness, and evolution were most needed in our world. Looking back, I see that my best, most expansive and creative thoughts did not come when I was hunched over a computer, or in focused thought, but rather lilted into my mind from the ether when I had completely let go of every intention, while flowing through my Tai Chi forms or in Sitting Qigong, Nei Gong, meditations.

Had I followed the Yang/controlled path of my life, perhaps pursuing a career in Sociology (my major at the university), and had not followed the wild seas and pathless tides that my Tai Chi and Qigong journey led me on, it would have seemed orderly, proper and practical. Much more practical than all the countless hours I spent learning and practicing Tai Chi and Qigong. I am not saying my formal education was not important. In fact, I also am not sure that I would have been able to comprehend how the microcosm of my Tai Chi and Qigong classes (where health professionals and people of all walks of life saw life changing benefit) related to the larger world, which ultimately led to my organizing World Tai Chi & Qigong Day. My sociology education at the university, like Taoist philosophy, was also about seeing the macrocosm of the world in the microcosmic experiences of individuals.

But Tai Chi and Taoist concepts of letting go, and feeling the flow of the Tao, enabled me to move beyond the self-doubt of considering, "What do Tai Chi and Taoist study offer my life?" I mean, it made no sense in the Yang logical world to pursue these fields of study, and to put the massive amount of time into them that I did. After all, I was a shipping clerk coming out of college when I began my Tai Chi and Qigong study, struggling to keep an expensive California house over our heads. 40 years ago there was not even the mountain of medical research there is today on the Internal Arts. Research that at least could have justified such a pursuit for the measurable benefits they give. It really seemed like a frivolous and huge waste of time. Or at least all the Yang, control, practical parts of my mind told me so. But so much has unfolded from following Lao Tzu's advice. Keeping to the Yin, the internal, the flow that cannot be seen, but can only be felt and resisted or flowed with.

I read that Gandhi once said, 'I have a really busy day today. I'll have to meditate more.' However, 40 years ago the "practicality of Internal Arts" wasn't apparent to most of the world, or to me really – it just "felt right." At the time, that was my only motivation. 40 years ago, only by diving into the ocean of mind-body practices over a period of years, could one "feel" the importance and practicality of them, *before* all the medical research came out over these decades. Today, it absolutely makes no sense at all that everyone on the planet is not already practicing Internal Arts, with what science now knows about their mental, emotional, and physical health benefits. For decades my life has been dedicated to making sure the world knows this. But it was the Yin experiences which made no sense, that I think kept me on a nebulous quest, a continuous journey down the nameless intangible path of the Internal Arts – starting with the angel's qigong lesson.

After my angelic experience with the "breathing lessons" 55 years ago, I remember how disappointed I had been, after waking up so excited to go to school, and show the other kids what the angel had taught me – how to fly. But then as I ran down the alley toward my school, taking a deep breath to lift up off the ground, I just came down with a squish in the mud puddle in the alley. I was so disappointed.

Today I realize that the "other kids" I was supposed to share my new awareness and excitement about the "breathing lessons" the angel had taught me were the people of planet Earth. All of God's children, living in an age of extreme stress. In changing times people need a model of "change" to get through, which is what Tai Chi and Qigong are – *models of change*, designed to help us relax and breathe through the strain of change. To loosen and allow changes to flow through us, physically, mentally, and emotionally. I have read psychologists who called Tai Chi a perfect model for observing the changes of life.

Over 50 years ago the angel had taught me that the world needed to unite our Yin creative open-minded world, where we are able to dream and open to wholly new ways of being, and where we are able to flow with the tides of change – with the Yang formed structural world. In order to enable us to actually physically create this new changing world, which we will need in these challenging times. The angel was teaching me that those two hemispheres (right brain and left brain) are connected by "the breath." Since that lesson from the angel so many decades ago, I studied all forms of meditation, and discovered that "the breath" is at the core of all types of meditation.

The breath is what unites our Yin and Yang consciousness and world, and the breath is what takes our Qigong and Tai Chi to that ethereal meditative level, where our arts become Internal, open to the unformed, the nebulous, the wellspring of all things. The 'creativity' that Einstein said was 'more important than knowledge.'

"Breath is the bridge which connects life to consciousness,
which unites your body to your thoughts."
-- Thich Nhat Hanh

"There is one way of breathing that is shameful and constricted. Then, there's another way: a breath of love that takes you all the way to infinity."
-- Rumi

I have come to realize that the Yin Yang dynamic is always at the source of vast possibilities.

I would look back and comprehend that my and my wife's lives had been an ultimate Yin Yang symbol. Me a small town Kansas boy, and her, a girl from the sprawling Chinese metropolis of Hong Kong, half a world away. Me, from the modern Western United States, and her the daughter of traditional Chinese parents who understood the tenets of a thousands-of-years-old traditional Chinese way of life. Our lives became the swirling white wave and black wave of the Yin Yang, as we struggled for 40 years to weave such different ways of life, ways of being, ways of seeing the world into one life. Our lives were the training ground for one day creating a very special book on Tai Chi. A book that would take the treasures of the East – my wife's family had helped me understand on a much deeper level – and explain them in simple, tangible, modern Western ways that a rural Kansas boy like myself could understand. In a way that would enable people all over the world in many cultures to comprehend them better.

Our ability to explain these complex Chinese concepts was refined so well because I, being a Kansas small town boy, understood as well as anyone how odd and intangible these Chinese mystical concepts seemed at first. It took me years to understand their wisdom, and without my wife's influence over the decades, would never have made the deep sense to me they do today. So again, the Taoist formula of the

Yin and the Yang, the interplay of my wife's traditional Chinese roots and my Yang Western, small-town struggle to understand them, was the genesis for a book that likely could not have been created in any other way.

When Macmillan Publishing in New York published my first book on Tai Chi, I was nervous about its release. It was unlike any other because it did not describe Tai Chi or Qigong or Taoism in traditional Chinese ways and contained very few Chinese words or labels. It was written from my own organic experience of over a decade, practicing and "feeling" Tai Chi, and being schooled in Chinese concepts, culture, and vision by my wife's constant presence and my effort to understand "her way of seeing the world."

It was written from my own Internal Arts Yin experience, and also from a lifetime of being exposed to Yin Eastern concepts that only a life with another human being who lived and breathed that reality, and who gently hammered Eastern lessons into my often closed and arrogant Western mind. The book could never have come from my Yang memorization of phrases or formulas I had read in books, or was exposed to only in classes. Because my book was so organic and nontraditional, I was afraid I would be eviscerated by traditionalists in the Tai Chi world.

Then, one of the first reader reviews I got was from the seminal All Forms Tai Chi Grand Champion of the United States, a Chinese Tai Chi master, named Master Hong Yijiao. She wrote that my book took the "best parts of Tai Chi," and explained difficult Chinese concepts in tangible ways that did not require the reader to have a grounding in Chinese culture or history in order to *get it*. I was vindicated! *What a relief!* I was further vindicated when my book was reviewed by the Team USA Senior Coach (Dr. Michael Steward, Sr.) who called it "visionary" and "life changing." This book, so far outside the Yang world of memorizing and regurgitating traditional explanations, could not have come without this global Yin and Yang fusion of my Yang-Western Kansas background, and my wife's Yin-traditional Chinese background. Or of our marriage, working out all the challenges of reconciling the

East and West in the microcosm of our own home, before then turning it over to the macrocosm of the Tai Chi world.

This Yin Yang formula would unfold more and more as my book's release would then help unfold what would become a worldwide event – World Tai Chi & Qigong Day.

For me and my wife, Tai Chi had become a common experience that enabled us to handle the storms of life. Storms that such a wild disparity of life experience would entail, weaving our Western and Eastern experiences of life in a more cohesive way, and giving us the stress management tools to allow that to happen.

[Photo courtesy of Blue Lotus Wellbeing Foundation www.mohamedessa.com]

World Tai Chi & Qigong Day 2016 celebration in Cairo, Egypt

Tai Chi became a wonderful source of our marriage's common ground. This microcosm of our common ground enabled a macrocosmic effect to unfold through us, as we organized people all over the world in over 80 countries to join together each year to celebrate World Tai Chi & Qigong Day, whose motto is "One World ... One Breath." People all across the planet would find common ground in Tai Chi and Qigong, across racial, ethnic, religious, and geo-political borders. And our marital training in international relations prepared us to be malleable enough to work with people all over the world. Two human beings could have never unfolded this in this way. It had to flow organically through us, if we were able to let go and allow space for it all to happen. The Internal Arts training we had was integral to that being possible.

Nearly 55 years after that angel gave me my first breathing lesson, my first Qigong lesson, and after my being so absolutely disappointed about being unable to fly when I ran to school, practicing the angel's breathing exercise to show the other kids how to fly, I was now flying with people all over the world, as we come together year after year to celebrate "One World … One Breath." That angel's vision actually did come to pass.

"As Tai Chi teachers we learn about the Tao, this field of existence where all things are connected. But as a Westerner it feels too intangible and unreal. Then we experience a synchronicity that is unexplainable, and it makes one wonder if the ancient Taoists were not actually seeing a deep reality.

Many years ago I was on a cruise in Egypt doing the 18 Taijiqigong in the morning on deck. A young man was putting the pillows on the longchairs, and

after a few days he said to me 'You look like an angel when you do that' ... and it was at that moment that I realized that when people watch someone do Tai Chi they can feel touched by an angel, and perhaps it was important for people to see Tai Chi.

Then, I discovered a global education project, called World Tai Chi & Qigong Day, which I would learn organized massive Tai Chi events in countries worldwide, and did mass publicity work to get the image of Tai Chi onto television screens worldwide and into the mind of humanity.

For me personally, you can imagine how stunning it was for me to learn just recently that World Tai Chi & Qigong Day's (WTCQD) Founder's vision of this global event--had come from an *angelic* experience the Founder had as a child—when it was a deckhand in Egypt who had inspired me to eventually become part of this global event when he said he felt like he was watching an angel when I did Tai Chi in the morning on the ship's deck.

To look back and see how all of this unfolded—my experience with the deckhand saying my Tai Chi looked like an angel, and my starting WTCQD events in Europe, which the event's Founder has told me inspired other events across Europe and the world—and learning that the entire global event had been originally inspired by the Founder's angelic experience—all resulting in a massive WTCQD happening spreading all across Europe, Asia, Oceania, North and South America, and Africa—makes one wonder if this concept of a field, the Tao that connects all minds and all things, is much more than just pretty Chinese poetry."
-- Hilda Cardinaels, Belgian Tai Chi teacher, and World Tai Chi & Qigong Day organizer in Belgium

---

You see, this is how the Tao works. It requires us to breathe and let go, in order to be able to follow a sense that is larger than we can hold or control in our linear Yang mind. It requires us to let the flow carry us on its tides using our Internal Arts practice to constantly let go of what we think should happen logically, when something larger is pulling us – calling us – even as it can't make logical sense at the time. And just as when the angel taught me to fly, and I got scared as I lifted off the ground and held my breath in fear (only to be reminded to "breathe and let go" by the angel), our entire lifetime of this Taoist journey was only made possible by continually practicing that angel's lesson, our Qigong lesson, of breathing through our fears.

It is vastly expensive to create a world event. Our lives have been a long journey of fear, breathing, letting go, and trusting enough to open to a flow we could not understand much of the time. We did not know that people all across the planet were also having a sense that something needed to come into being worldwide. We could only follow our inner flow that often made no logical sense at the time.

This can only be felt, and surrendered to, not worked out mentally. Things larger than we are capable of envisioning can have space to unfold in us, to unfold us, when we play at the arts of letting go over years and decades. This is the way of the Tao.

Over 5 decades later, following years and years and years of Taoist and meditative study, to be here today is a real testament to the way of the Tao – flying together with the world, flying on the breathing techniques an angel taught me as a young boy (that I would expand on in a Qigong class as a young man), and that would enable possibilities to unfold through me.

And each year people all over the planet Earth, from the Philippines to Singapore, from Brazil to Mexico, from Canada to Russia, and 80 nations in between, people post banners with World Tai Chi & Qigong Day's motto "One World … One Breath," and people all over the world breathe together on the same day under those banners.

This event that I organized nearly two decades ago is a global flower that was planted in my mind 55 years ago as a boy by an angel. Who introduced me to the tools that would enable me to open to the Tao. The nebulous, then unknowable, and its petals have spread across the planet at all levels of society, with the help of people all over the planet opening to investing themselves in similar ways.

It has inspired health ministries and sports ministries and parks ministries and universities and hospitals to help and support these events, as well as consulates and embassies from India to China, Italy, and the United States. Government bodies all over the world have officially recognized and supported events. When the *Harvard Medical*

School Guide to Tai Chi was published, it recognized World Tai Chi & Qigong Day's efforts as a testament to how widely these mind-body arts have spread around the world.

Several Harvard Medical School researchers held a "Tai Chi for Health" symposium on World Tai Chi & Qigong Day, to commemorate the global event. The U.S. National Institutes of Health once paid for airline tickets meant to fly me to speak at their Mind Body Week in Washington, D.C. on how Tai Chi and Qigong could profoundly reduce health costs in America and worldwide, if taught en masse to our population, through education, healthcare, senior care, and the like.

I realize now, that angel 55 years ago who gave me breathing lessons, *was indeed* preparing me to fly. But not the way a six year old boy could have ever comprehended.

[Photos courtesy of Blue Lotus Wellbeing Foundation www.mohamedessa.com]

World Tai Chi & Qigong Day celebrations are a worldwide wave of events all held on the last Saturday of April in 100s of cities in 80 nations

That angel was teaching me how Qigong breathing can help us drop the anchors of stress in our mind, heart, and body, in order to feel lighter and move more lightly in our lives. And its lessons set the stage for me to literally take off into the air, traveling to Australia, Brazil, and

Africa, places I never would have been without the angel's lesson. In a way traveling there to help teachers all over the world, to spread the angel's breathing lesson, the Internal Arts.

Now I am able to tell all the other kids at school about the breathing lessons. Only the classroom is the entire planet, and the other students are all of the Earth's children.

I have found that when we surrender open to these currents of energy flowing through us at times in our lives, they are most often much larger experiences than we can comprehend at the time they happen to us.

They have to unfold through our lives. Like an unfolding flower does not bloom at once. It has to unfold in all its glory over time. We cannot demand these insights, we cannot force them into existence, we can only surrender and open. And then continue surrendering and opening, to allow more and more to unfold through us. Things bigger than we can understand at any given moment.

"Your organizing of this global event has been very helpful in gaining media attention for the benefits of Qi Gong & Tai Chi and in creating awareness of our school and classes. New people come to our World Tai Chi & Qi Gong Day event every year."
-- Howard Fraracci, Qi Gong teacher, Toronto, Ontario, Canada

"Our Tai Chi programs continue to grow and our numbers of Tai Chi Schools continue to grow at a phenomenal rate and I feel your efforts are fueling this growth worldwide and we are all in awe of what the World Tai Chi & Qigong Day has done."
-- Dave Pickens, National Chairman Chinese Martial Arts Division United States Amateur Athletic Union

---

I see Tai Chi and Qigong and the Internal Arts as profound sciences that foster one's ability to surrender open to the flow of the Tao that courses through the universe beneath the surface of the manifest.

They are simple and fun, and profoundly healthful, and as deep as the deepest ocean and as high as the highest science.

Yin Arts – Internal Arts

Thinking is Yang, feeling is Yin.

Looking back at my 55 year journey leading from an angel in Western Kansas to a Taoist Temple in Hong Kong, and eventually across the planet, from Australia, to China, Brazil, United Kingdom, and across Africa – was a struggle to learn how to *feel* my way through life, rather than just thinking my way through it.

You see, I never could have *thought* my way through it, because so many of the things that made all of this happen seemed absolutely mad at the time. They only make sense in retrospect. Retrospect is so often the *only way* following "the sense of the Tao" ever makes logical, linear sense.

He has staked his savings on setting up the website (www.worldtaichiday.org) and getting everything organised -- the fax bill alone last month was about 15,000 dollars: what return can he possibly expect?

"I don't know: I have no idea," [Bill Douglas] admitted on the phone from his home town of Kansas City. "I just know I had to try it."
--South China Morning Post, Hong Kong, April 1, 2000

This is the Taoist way, because you can only feel the Tao, you can never intellectually understand it. That was what Lao Tzu meant by warning that the true Tao could never be named.

How do we feel our way through life? I can't tell you how, but for me, Nei Gong meditation and Tai Chi were absolutely critical to my being able to do so. You see, we have a tendency to hear something, or be told something, or mentally decide something, based on "facts that make sense." And that decides our path toward where we are going. Even though we have a sense at times that something else is calling us. That we have another path to follow. Some might call it a hunch.

I have found that it is what "excites" me, the paths or projects which lift me and light me, is an indicator of when I am flowing with the Tao. I seem to have endless energy and inspiration when I am flowing with the Tao, and huge tasks start to seem almost effortless. This seems to be how I navigate it like a sailor tacking an ocean breeze. I am not saying that this journey has been easy and that it hasn't been exhausting over the years at time. I am not a perfect sailor, and I cannot always perfectly tack the winds. But what I do know is that I have crossed vast oceans that would have been too hard to circumnavigate, had it not been for the winds that I have been wise enough to feel and to flow with.

In this journey I had to learn how to be a professional writer for starters. I had no formal training and was a lousy English student in school. Only after a second angelic experience in my early 20s would I become a writer, specifically due to that experience (more on that later). I had to train myself as a writer in order to eventually become a *professional* writer (which is way harder than it might seem if you haven't done it). The Yin flow of the Tao pushed me in that direction, then I had to go with that flow and do the Yang work to realize it.

Then I had to let the waves and currents wash me on their tides, as World Tai Chi & Qigong Day was born from my writing, evolving into an internationally published Tai Chi book. That wave washed me on another tide, and I had to learn a *host of skills;* how to be a webmaster, how to do mass media promotion, how to do Photoshop, how to produce video. Skills that often take a lifetime to acquire, and I had to make it happen over a fairly short number of years, in order to keep up with the rapid growth and expanding demands of World Tai Chi & Qigong Day. Keep in mind I had to do all of this in my spare time, outside of my Tai Chi school, which was how I scraped my living. While doing all of this international organizing as a volunteer.

Of course, learning how to teach Tai Chi in the beginning was a huge task, and the prerequisite to all of this. And because I only decided to teach years after leaving my teacher in California to move to Kansas City, I had to really learn how to do this teaching part pretty much on my own, by the seat of my pants. I was swirling in a wave. A neighbor asked me to teach them the Tai Chi they saw me playing in my back yard, and then others wanted to learn. This led me to rent a church basement, then Yoga studios, and eventually I was commissioned to teach in hospitals and corporations, and then other currents swept me in other directions. I had to surrender to what felt like chaos, letting go constantly, and flowing with swirling changing waves welling up under and around me.

The waves washed me and my teaching into hospitals, corporations, and then drug and prison programs, troubled youth programs, churches, synagogues, and public schools and special education institutions. All of this was preparing me for something I could never have envisioned or planned out logically. You see, in order for World Tai Chi & Qigong Day to become what it would one day become, I had to learn how to pioneer getting Tai Chi into society at all levels. This would eventually be the thrust of World Tai Chi & Qigong Day organizing efforts, to help teachers worldwide expand mind body arts into society at all levels. But all of this preparation occurred "before" I even had the idea of World Tai Chi & Qigong Day – I had to go with what "felt right" even as it seemed like chaos at the time.

This was years before Tai Chi was being brought into these types of settings. Before a lot of the hard science had validated Tai Chi, for companies and hospitals and schools justifying bringing Tai Chi into their offices and classrooms. It was a hard row to hoe back then – I had to learn how to be a promoter and media director. Had I not pioneered this expansion of Tai Chi into these new arenas personally, how could I have ever been able to create the tutorials for teachers worldwide, to replicate what we had done, and get Tai Chi into mass media worldwide?

I am not saying I was the only pioneer expanding Tai Chi at that level in those early years. But what I am saying is that no one to my knowledge was doing it on such a broad scale at all levels of society. And there was no one there to show me how to do it, which is why I worked so hard for years to provide free resources to Tai Chi teachers worldwide, via the World Tai Chi & Qigong Day website and global newsletter. I did this so other teachers could follow our example, and not have to reinvent the wheel and waste precious time, at a time when Internal Arts were so profoundly needed by global society.

This all required me to follow this constant flow of hunches, or nudges, that I couldn't understand at the time. Looking back, it all makes such sense, like it was all skillfully and brilliantly built step-by-step to spread all around the world. But when I was in the middle of all of this it just seemed crazy at times, yet I could not resist doing it. If you ever watched "Close Encounters of the 3rd Kind," you may remember a scene where actor Richard Dreyfus's character has a vision, an image, in his head that he does not understand. But it is itching his brain, and it needs to be made manifest. He begins to mold his mashed potatoes at dinner in a shape he can't quite get. He begins to draw sketches that he can't quite complete, and finally he begins to shovel dirt into his living room and pull shrubs from his garden, throwing them through the window into his living room, as he struggles to shape this vision gnawing at his mind. He finally completes it, and in the background you see on his television screen an image of a rugged peak in Wyoming, and you realize that this is what he has been trying to shape and create. His mind just couldn't bring it in to focus. Everyone thought he was mad.

I have to be honest, at times I felt mad as well, back when I was spending *thousands of dollars* on global media outreach, to get the media to pay attention to World Tai Chi & Qigong Day events all over the planet. I was faxing media in Russia, Egypt, Hong Kong, all over Europe, all over South America, Australia and New Zealand, and connecting them with teachers and schools in those nations, to help them get media coverage for their events. World Tai Chi & Qigong Day had no dues, we had no way of supporting such efforts at the time.

[Photo credit, Ahmed Shaaban from Blue Lotus Wellbeing Foundation]
World Tai Chi & Qigong Day 2016. Cairo, Egypt.

A rational Yang mind would have spent those precious dollars in his hometown in Kansas City promoting his own classes, when those classes were barely generating enough income to pay the mortgage payments and food for his young family. It took a major sense of surrender and opening to let the Tao lead us to pour precious resources into promoting "other schools'" and "other teachers'" events. And doing this in countries I had not even heard of, before landing in the center of creating a World Tai Chi & Qigong Day, because the idea "came to me in a meditation." A South China Morning Post news reporter who interviewed me in 2001, calling me from Hong Kong on the telephone, asked me what return I thought I could get from this huge investment. I replied, "I have no idea. I only knew I had to try it."

That was the actions of someone in a Yin mode, flowing on a current he could not explain in words, but only "feel" the flow of, as he surrendered to it. To a Yang mind it looked insane. I won't lie to you, I felt that way more than once, but I didn't quit – in a way, I *couldn't* quit, an unseen current was pulling me. Something about all of this deeply "resonated within me." This wasn't the first time I had taken a leap like this and felt this resonation, this flow, that didn't make Yang rational sense at the time.

When I began teaching Tai Chi as a full time business, I was frightened as I resigned from a solid corporate job with solid steady paychecks, and solid health and other benefits.

I walked away from security and then became a very hard worker, flowing with ideas for flyers, and how to market classes, and ideas and thoughts that just kept coming. I was electric, more creative than I had ever been working at all the corporations I had worked at over the course of my life, before becoming a professional Tai Chi teacher. Something about this path "resonated" within me. It clicked, and I knew it was the way to go for me, even though it scared the hell out of me. I had fears and doubts about walking away from a steady solid corporate occupation with medical and sick days. But what drew me and excited me was so attractive that it overrode my fears and trepidations. I was a sailor tacking the winds, feeling within rather than being driven from without. Without a decade of Tai Chi, Qigong and Taoist practice, I don't think I could have felt it that powerfully. And even if I had, I think the stress of it all would have torn me up.

I wasn't entirely secure in this Yin internal. At times I would feel stuck and uninspired and in doubt. But then often at those times a student might linger after class and confide to me some amazing health benefit they had gotten from Tai Chi. Or some huge insight about state of being they had gotten from our Nei Gong meditations in class. These events would spur me on. The Yang external world and the Yin internal world began to collaborate, in overlapping waves. There would be synchronous signs in the Yang outside world to validate my internal Yin hunches, senses and cues, pushing me to do certain things. My life became trying to tune into a certain frequency, and my entire being was the radio receiver. Every sense, mental, emotional, and physical was how I would feel the music, when I tuned into it, or the static when I was off track. I felt it in my state of well-being or in my feelings of disturbance and dis-ease.

It was like teaching Tai Chi had struck a cosmic string that vibrated at the right frequency for me. Maybe that Taoist monk in the temple in Hong Kong over a decade before had heard that frequency in some way when reading my life with the I Ching (The Book of Changes) and informing me that I would become a teacher many years before I would know it.

Tai Chi teaching took me into another plane, another realm of consciousness, where the lessons flowed through me as I relaxed out of the way and allowed them passage. My classes became a portal for taking students to "another state of consciousness." I did and do offer Yang explanations and instruction in Tai Chi and Qigong techniques, but the overarching flow is Yin. I take students on a journey of the mind to other planes of consciousness. It is as if I did not choose teaching, rather teaching was a wave that welled up and washed me, and I let go and went for a ride upon it.

When I was teaching a Tai Chi Meditation seminar in Australia years ago, my host, a wonderful Tai Chi teacher named Bev Abela nudged my wife and remarked to Angela as I started my seminar, "Look at him, he's in a zone." When *in the zone,* I let go of formal lesson plans and go Yin, becoming a vessel, often not quite knowing what is going to come out of my mouth from moment to moment – surrendering to the flow of the Tao washing through me.

Last week a man started my hospital Tai Chi Meditation class and I was in "the flow" in a big way that day. He had studied for the Jesuit priesthood as a young man and discovered meditation along the way. In the midst of the class he exclaimed, "I have been involved in meditation for 40 years, and I just have to say that I have never experienced anything like this class. Something big is happening in here!" When we flow in the Tao, huge and vast things can unfold through us.

How did that Taoist monk in Hong Kong see this in me with such certainty so many years ago, long before I did? Some physicists theorize that "all possible realities exist, all the time." And the reality which becomes real is simply which one our consciousness resonates to, and chooses on some level. Einstein was convinced that Mozart's music was so perfect and organic that it could not have possibly been "made up" by Mozart. That Mozart must have "opened up" to music that already existed in the universe.

Bob Dylan and other great artists believe this is the case as well. These artists do not believe that they, themselves are capable of such writing. They feel they are opening to a flow that passes through them. I think we all have that capacity. Although it may not be music or art, we may open to innovative possibilities in our work or in all levels of life. It could take on any form, maybe you are destined to be the ultimate parent who finds your rhythm in parenthood, and your offspring is destined to change the world. Or maybe your engineering work is leading to something that will ripple out in vast ways. We know we are in the Tao when it flows through us like a wellspring. This is the Yin way, the Taoist way. And the Tai Chi way ultimately, when we become so proficient at our Tai Chi that we can let go and allow it to flow through us. I think that this is what Tai Chi can prepare us for. To become more proficient at relaxing out of the way of larger possibilities than we could imagine on our own, or hold in our current state of mind. Possibilities that are calling to us, pulling us towards them, if we can let go of our grip on the banks of the world and let the current pull us.

The Yin comes from within with information, or nudges of emotion or feelings. Being able to "hear" the quiet whispers of our internal awareness helps us tune into the flow, the Tao, the current carrying us to where we can be most effective in our actions, our lives, our world.

When Pushing Hands in Tai Chi, we establish a rhythm and flow with our Push Hands partner, advancing not with arm exertion, but with an unbendable arm flowing with Qi. The force of our advance or push is really from the Dan Tien, our center of being, and not the arm or shoulder. Then we recede, yielding out of the way as our partner advances, giving them nothing to push against.

As we become proficient at Push Hands, we can in a sense "feel inside our partner's body," as we push into them. When there is nothing to push against, we know our partner is relaxed and yielding. However, when we feel resistance, we know that our partner is not relaxed, and is vulnerable to being pushed off balance. At that moment it takes hardly any effort to send them off balance. But if you pushed on them when they were yielding it would be much harder to do so.

Tai Chi is at its most physical core – engineering. Master Henry Look is one of the senior masters in the Guang Ping Yang Style of Tai Chi, a direct student of Master Kuo Lien-Ying. Sifu Look was a professional architect when he was on the cover of Tai Chi Magazine. He said that Tai Chi is high level engineering, in that it is about learning how to do the most, with the least effort.

When we "Gather Qi," or "Stand Universal Post," it is an ancient form of biofeedback. We listen inside ourselves for the sensations that tell us how to correct our posture, and to let our muscles and body sink and settle and let go of strain. That is why over time one can Stand Post for longer and longer periods of time. When I was young, I thought Standing Post was a macho act of masochism, thinking he who could suffer the longest was the Standing Post Winner. But now I see that it is not about suffering and pain. It is about learning how to "let go," and "feeling the flow," as we breathe and let tight spots sigh and open to the flow or radiance of Qi. This is done by first learning how to "turn within" and to "feel" inside ourselves. Once we feel inside, then we can begin to untangle the tight spots we hold.

Push Hands is an external sense of biofeedback, just as Standing Post is internal sense. While Taoism is about getting a sense of the flow of the larger universe passing through us, and feeling when its flow hitches. This can provide a sense that we are going the wrong direction. Taoism, meditation, and Tai Chi can help us sense this early, before big problems result from that wrong path.

Learning this more subtle sense of self via Internal (Universal Post) and

External (Push Hands) can also help us find shortcuts in life, by feeling a sense of effortless flow when things are going the right way – or pressure and tension when things are going off course. Tai Chi and Push Hands can teach us how to have the "biggest impact" with the "least effort," when we are able to "feel" our partner at their most vulnerable point when they tighten. If your partner was not tightened and vulnerable it would take a lot of effort to push them off balance. But, when you sense that "hitch" when they are not yielding and are bracing, then the smallest effort could send them flying off balance. Okay, so Push Hands can show us how to have a physical impact with other people, but what about life in general? Can Push Hands help us flow with the Tao in our larger life? Yes!

Universal Post, Standing Post at World Tai Chi & Qigong Day Headquarters

Standing Post is a Yin practice. "Allowing" the Qi to flow through us, showing us where we are holding on ... so that we can breathe and play at the art of *letting go* ...

Here's one vivid example of how you can "feel" your way through issues and life decisions. When I was a boy in Cub Scouts, a man came to our Scout meeting and showed us some Yoga techniques that amazed us. He also showed us how to "muscle test," whereby first he had each of us hold a cigarette in one hand. Then, holding that arm out to our side at shoulder height, we were told to resist as the man pushed down on our arm. We had no power or strength and he pushed our arm down easily when the cigarette was in our hand. Then, we put the cigarette down, and held a piece of fresh fruit in our hand instead, and he had a much more difficult time pushing our arm down. We were stronger.

This gives you an idea of why the subtle internal awareness that Tai Chi, Qigong, Universal Post and Push Hands practices cultivate in us can help us do more than just physically perform better. Playing at and practicing at this "internal awareness" that the Internal Arts cultivate in us can help us attune to a higher-lighter state of awareness and wisdom that we all hold within – if we slow down and learn how to listen. Tai Chi and Qigong are profound tools to practice slowing down and listening.

When I was a young man, I spent thousands of hours on street corners and going door to door, trying to awaken people to unnecessary suffering in the world. I was doing human rights work after serving in a Salvadoran and Guatemalan Refugee camp in the 1980s. I also worked to educate the public about environmental issues that were causing suffering to many because of pollution problems.

Bill Douglas in Salvadoran Refugee Camp

Over the years I began to realize that when I did such work, I was not really converting anyone with the information I shared about such issues. What I was really doing was trying to connect with people who already agreed with me. If someone's heart was closed to the suffering of others, no amount of information would open their heart. Eventually I felt that hitch, that sense that this was not my path. It felt too hard, too ineffective.

Eventually, over the years, political work became less and less of a draw to me, even though I still wanted to help others who were needlessly suffering in the world. I felt a sense of the flow of the Tao when I learned that new scientific research on mind-body meditative practices like I taught, showed that they could actually physically enlarge the "empathy/compassion" part of the brain, when people practiced these meditative arts. I had experienced it in my life. Mind-body practices made me more civil, more open to other's stories, and more empathetic to what others deal with. Many of my students have experienced similar changes in themselves after practicing the Internal Arts for a while.

I wanted to help alleviate suffering, but sensed within (because of my Internal Arts and Taoist training) that issue politics was not flowing with the Tao (for me at that time. It doesn't mean that's true for anyone else). But, I did feel a sense of flow and opportunity opening, when I learned of the effect of meditation on enlarging people's empathy/compassion part of the brain.

So my internal awareness from Tai Chi, Qigong, and Taoist practice helped me feel a door close and another door, or flow, open. My Tai Chi training and my Push Hands training had also shown me that we can attune within to realize at what point, and in what way, we can have the "biggest impact" with the "least effort." Like when we can send a Push Hands partner off balance, when we feel their tightness or vulnerability.

My life turned less and less to issue politics, where the energy or flow seemed diminished or blocked, and more and more to expanding awareness of mind-body Internal Arts practices like Nei Gong, Tai Chi, and Qigong. It was a short cut, more effective, more powerful, and demanding less energy.

Rather than beating my head against a wall, spending my life futilely trying to get people who had little empathy and compassion for others' suffering to act on information I shared with them about that suffering, I instead spent my life sharing Internal Arts meditative tools in every way I could. I taught in corporations, in hospitals, in schools, in prisons and drug rehabilitation programs, and more. I saw students become more empathetic and compassionate people over the months and years of their Tai Chi Meditation journey.

The Tao offers solutions that are multidimensional, not linear. Complex patterns can come together. For example, some people do Tai Chi to improve their balance, and that's all they want from it. However, over time they see not only their balance improve, but they see their high blood pressure become normalized. Or they need less or no more insulin because their Type 2 Diabetes improved or went away. So, as I was teaching thousands of people Internal Arts for health reasons, or drug or prison rehabilitation reasons – many of these people were also getting larger empathy/compassion parts of the brain. I was contributing to a more compassionate world in this way, having the "most impact," with the "least effort." This is the Tai Chi way. This is the Taoist way.

Ancient Chinese Tai Chi masters were have said to warn students that, "The mirror is your enemy." This was a warning not to let the Yang, the external mind, rule your Tai Chi. They urged us to not look at ourselves from the outside in, as most of the world does, and which is why the world is so obsessed with "the way they look" as opposed to "the way they feel." The fitness crazes of past decades with mottos like "no pain, no gain" were the embodiment of a Yang concept, striving to "look good," rather than to "feel good." Even this becomes psychologically twisted, as the "way people feel" often depends on "the way they look to others," rather than how they feel within. The masters urged us to "feel the sensation of within," and to let that be the guide to our Tai Chi, rather than the way we look from the outside-in-via-the-mirror of the world's opinion of us.

Again, Universal Post, Standing Post, or Gathering Qi is a stance that is common to all styles of Tai Chi. At its core, it is bio-feedback, "feeling within" and allowing our body to adjust posture, to breathe, to let go, to take pressure off the body and being. This internal approach to "feeling within" is the Yin approach. Using the mirror in external observation of ourselves is the Yang approach. The world is obsessed with Yang approaches. The internal, the Yin, this is the way of the universe. This is how we access deeper truth.

When we begin Tai Chi study, we "hold" postures. I heard about a Tai Chi master in China who would have his students hold out their arms and he would walk by and push their arm down. The students would either "hold" their arm stiff in resistance, or would "pull" their arms down as he pushed on them. He would correct them not to do either. He wanted them to "surrender" their arm to gravity's pull.

In time, after more and more practice, or more accurately, after we experience more "playing Tai Chi," we know our postures so well that we begin to surrender, and to "sink" into the postures. Again, this is an act of surrender, of letting the forms flow through us, and surrendering every cell of our being to gravity, to sink onto the Vertical Axis. The rod of energy that flows from 12 and 1/2 feet above us, elongating and lifting us weightlessly through our movements, and also down through the center of our being to 12 and 1/2 feet below us, rooting us into the Earth.

At first we imagine these concepts, the Vertical Axis lengthening and rooting us, the concept of "sinking" onto the Vertical Axis, and surrendering into the movements. This imagining is an act of will and effort in our mind and body, and is therefore Yang, External, Masculine consciousness. It is a metaphor for the world we walk in, its rules, its laws, its mores, its restrictions.

Tai Chi and Qigong are the Internal Arts, the Yin Arts. They help us learn to become unmoored from the Yang world, to float on the nebulous and pathless seas of our inner being. To experience consciousness undefined by words, unlimited by the past. Lao Tzu told us that the true way of the universe, the underlying energetic flow of all things, could never be named. For the naming itself limits and defines, putting fences around that which is undefinable, too vast, too nebulous, too new and unconceived of.

But over time, we know the Yang, the masculine, *the forms*. And then we can surrender into the Yin *formless* effortless sinking from leg to leg, movement to movement, being flowed by our Dan Tien. This is when our Tai Chi becomes less of an "exercise" and more "playing" Tai Chi. When we let go of control and begin to slip into the Yin art, the yielding, we surrender out of the way of the movements flowing through us.

The breath – *breathes us*. The movements – move us ... as we relax out of the way.

I emphasize the word "play" and "playing" Tai Chi, because when I first traveled to Hong Kong so long ago, I had been "working" very hard for many months, to learn my Tai Chi forms to impress my Chinese mother-in-law upon my arrival.

One day my brother-in-law, Sammy Wong, who was also our informal tour guide on the trip, because he had a car and knew Hong Kong like the back of his hand, drove us past a park near Hong Kong Stadium in the Causeway Bay area of Hong Kong Island. I saw people doing what I suspected was Tai Chi as we passed by the park, and I asked Sammy, "What are they doing?"

He glanced over and replied, "Oh, they're playing Tai Chi."

You see, after all my hard work on Tai Chi in the recent months to prepare for my Hong Kong trip, I thought he was dismissing what they were doing as just "goofing around at Tai Chi," and not really being real Tai Chi enthusiasts. But what I would learn, through the course of that Hong Kong trip, was that this is what Chinese people call Tai Chi exercise. Not "working out," but "playing" Tai Chi. Work, you see, is Yang, analytical, effort, while playing is very Yin.

Lao Tzu told us that all things are done when it seems as though we are doing nothing, that great accomplishment comes out of non-effort, He told us to keep to the Yin side of reality because that is where all things are born from.

You can see how this trip was turning my consciousness upside down and inside out, and would lay the groundwork for a whole new way of approaching Tai Chi. And in fact for a whole new approach to life, a Taoist and Tai Chi way of life.

I got into a virulent argument on the Internet one day in a Tai Chi chatroom, because when I made this point about Chinese people "playing Tai Chi," rather than working at it, someone claimed that I had it all wrong, because he saw Tai Chi as work. That was his approach – very serious, very precise, very Yang. He said that what Chinese people meant was that it was like a sport, like "playing" baseball. One would say ball players are playing baseball, but still working at it.

I live in Kansas City, and as many of you may know, our Kansas City Royals (who we are very proud of) became world champions, winning the World Series in 2015. If you follow the Royals, you know that they play at a level that is heartbreakingly beautiful at times, exhibiting ballet-esque feats that would put Baryshnikov to shame. What announcers always remark on is "how much fun" this team seems to have, and how much they "enjoy playing" the game, and many sports reporters attribute their success to that "playing" of the game. Remember Mohammed Ali, and how he would play in the ring. Yes, he and the Royals practiced and practiced and practiced, but they were very playful, and that Yin playfulness seemed to spawn a spontaneity that allowed a higher level of possibility to flow through them.

So when I read Lao Tzu's Taoist admonition about how getting the most done feels like we are doing nothing, it resonated with me, because I was just at that point of proficiency in my Tai Chi practice. When it was becoming "play," and my Tai Chi Long Form, which had seemed to take forever when I was in the Yang learning mode, went by in the blink of an eye, when I moved to the level of "playing" Tai Chi. I was constantly making adjustments in posture and loosening, but it wasn't conscious, it was surrendering to a total immersion in the pleasure of the movements, the adjustments happening on a higher level than my linear mind was capable of.

This is the Yin way, the Taoist approach to Tai Chi. This is the goal of Tai Chi. As we rise to this level everything in our lives becomes more playful.

When I finally began to learn how to "play" Tai Chi, my biggest regret was that I hadn't played at it more all along. I realized that Tai Chi had NEVER been hard, what made it hard was all the sharp rigid tangles I had held in my head. And I realized that those same tangles had not only held my Tai Chi progress back, but had held back every aspect of my life. Had I held my Tai Chi practice lightly, had fun, and played at it, I would have absorbed information so much faster and easier. This is what the Internal Arts offer the world, the ability to evolve, learn, make adjustments more easily and quickly.

One thing, looking back, is that I was constantly castigating myself when my balance was off, or I would forget a movement, etc. That self-criticism was a tendency I had that held my whole life back, and I see that in new students all the time. When they learn some new aspect or subtlety or level of Tai Chi, they have to make themselves "wrong," for having not known that all along.

The more we can let go of that tendency, the more easily we can open to new information, and evolve, not just in our Tai Chi play, but as a society and world. And in a world changing as fast as this one, this is a skill the world desperately needs. When we let go of fear of failure unfolding creativity can flow through us.

Recently I confided to one of my advanced Tai Chi classes that when I enter a class, I completely let go of any game-plan or lesson plan I had held in my mind, while meditating in my car before entering the class. I let go of everything and open to the field and to the class's field, to allow the Tao or flow of energy that I do not control, but is created by that class and my Yin flowing nature, and by my student's Yin flowing nature, to take me on its currents.

When I feel that sense of unhinging and flowing, I open my car door and enter the class. I enter as fresh and effervescent and open as any student in the class, and let the class unfold, often cuing off of student's comments, or other things that lilt into the experience from within me as well. The class becomes organic, spontaneous, flowing in the nebulous, the Yin.

To be fair to new teachers, I have not always taught like this. In the beginning years I often planned things on the way to class, or days before even, because when we first start teaching we are afraid we might lose track of where we are, and look like a deer in the headlights, losing face in front of our students.

But now, partly because of years of practice, and partly because of my age, but also largely due to the brain changes that Tai Chi Meditation has on us, I do not fear looking like a fool. In fact some of the best classes we have are when I at some point look like a fool, and the class has a big uproarious laugh. That is the Taoist way, the Tai Chi way. It takes pressure off the class, and it takes pressure off of me as a teacher. Students no longer "feel dumb" when they forget a Tai Chi form, or lose track of where they are, and I can relax because it is okay if I look like a fool. Lao Tzu told me so.

Lao Tzu told us that when in the Tao he appeared "dull," while everyone else seemed to have purpose, and that he was alone drifting on the waves of the ocean of existence.

When I let go, and allow the Tai Chi class to flow through me, and through all of us in the class, those are the classes when huge things happen. When deep connections are made, and when we all remember that we are "playing" at Tai Chi. It is the Taoist way, it is the Tai Chi way.

Angela Oi Yue Wong, WTCQD Founder

I have learned this in many ways and different angles from teachers all around the planet. I used to teach in a very Yang way, only imparting knowledge to students without "being with them," in a Yin way. Many people helped me understand this Yin way, evolving my teaching to be "with" students, rather than solely focused on the Yang approach of just imparting knowledge to students. These people included the Australian teacher, Bev Abela, and Elizabeth Keith (a teacher in Phoenix, Arizona), and two Chinese teachers in Hong Kong (Master Luk and Olive Hui). And of course also my wife, Angela Oi Yue Wong who is from Hong Kong as well.

As you know by now, the Yin is the feminine in Taoist philosophy and the Yang is masculine. The concept is that we all have both Yin and Yang, masculine and feminine aspects, which is not about sexuality, but an approach to life. However, I do think that it is worth noting here that we are now experiencing a rise of female masters in our lifetime in Tai Chi, an art dominated by masculine Yang energy through its history. Until just now, in our lifetimes, and we are witnessing a very interesting positive healing effect on Tai Chi, as it has on my own practice and life.

A wholeness is being created as women take their place worldwide in these arts. Their impact is massive, and will unfold the Internal Arts' petals of evolution into the future in subtle yet powerful ways, that we cannot fully comprehend at this time. The Tao seeks balance. The Yin Yang, the Tai Chi symbol, is a symbol of the power of balance. Our world is coming into balance, and it will improve the Tai Chi for all of us.

I wish I could acknowledge all the women teachers and masters here who have transformed Tai Chi toward a Yin balance: Effie Chow (Founder of the World Congress on Qigong in San Francisco); U.S. All Forms Tai Chi Champion, Hong Yijao in Seattle; my own teacher Jais Booth in California; Judith Trethway who invited me to her program she taught at Folsom Prison; Hilda Cardinaels in Belgium; Margaret Reeves; Dr. Aihan Kuhn; Barbara Eisner; Peggy Wheeler in Topeka, Kansas; Alexia Rees in New York; and Barbara Grinter, Tina Webb, Sally Gordon, and Deb in my own Tai Chi classes.

I regret leaving out so many other formative female presences in the Tai Chi world, but please accept my humble bow here. Know that you and what you bring to this art is profoundly important, and appreciated by all of us, affecting countless generations in the future.

But, as I mentioned before, the Yin and Yang are not about sex, but rather a way of approaching the world. Just as women can have a Yang approach to life, men can be a force of Yin healing and compassion in the world. Master Wu and Professor Jose Milton de Olivera in Brasilia, Brazil come to mind. Their gentle healing approach to the Internal Arts has been a huge inspiration to me and to people around the world. Roger Jahnke, a co-founder of the National Qigong Association; Ariel Ondoua Betti Adolphe, a Tai Chi teacher from Cameroon, Africa, a force of nature spreading Tai Chi and meditation across the African continent; Master Li Junfeng, who extolled me to organize World Tai Chi & Qigong Day for "love"; Donald and Cheryl Rubbo in California; Ken Ryan in Maine; Dave Pickens in Austin; Dr. Shin Lin in California; Tai Chi legend David-Dorian Ross; Dr. Peter Wayne, author of *The Harvard Medical School Guide to Tai Chi;* Mohamed Essa in Cairo, Egypt; Dr. Robert Woodbine in Harlem, NY; Professor William Tsang at the Hong Kong Polytechnic University Tai Chi Research Lab; Dr. Pete Gryffin with the Metarobic Institute, and so many more I can't mention here, are also great contributors to this Yin healing wave of today's evolving Internal Arts.

If you know of a teacher I left out, who is influential in realizing the larger social and world vision of the Internal Arts as healing agents in the world, on your local level or on a global scale, please do not think I slighted them purposefully. Send me info (see my contact information in back of this book) and I will do my best to acknowledge them in our global weekly World Tai Chi & Qigong Day Ezine email newsletter: "All Things Tai Chi & Qigong," which goes out to thousands in the global Tai Chi and Qigong community around the planet each week.

Left Brain-Yang ... Right Brain-Yin

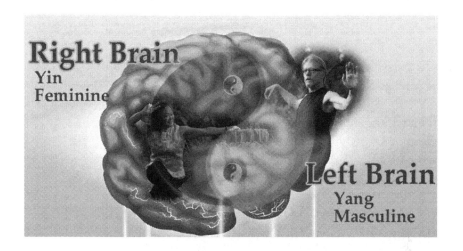

Lao Tzu's Tao te Ching, I have found, is the closest our left brain consciousness can come to a right brain experience, as the left brain reads the lines of Taoist poetry. Reading you see, is a left brain activity. Words are processed by the left brain, and Lao Tzu wrote that the true Tao cannot be put into words. However, the Tao te Ching is not written in a linear left brain sense making way. It is poetry, and poetry is the closest one can come to a right brain Yin experience with the written word.

In organizing World Tai Chi & Qigong Day, I have discovered that an inordinate number of Tai Chi teachers are also *poets*. I have come to understand why through my Tai Chi teaching. As teachers, we are constantly trying to use "words" to convey "sensations and feelings" we experience during Tai Chi and meditation. This forces us to become poets. Poetry is the art of using words to, not describe a feeling one has, but to actually "convey" that feeling into another human being. The words may not even make logical sense, but if they trigger that sensation in another, then the poetry is successful.

In this chapter, I will offer my own humble attempt to provide you with such an experience of "feeling" rather than "thinking about" feeling.

Here is where Tai Chi becomes Ch'an, *just being*, a transcendental experience that cannot be "figured out," it can only be witnessed as it passes through our consciousness in its own nebulous way.

Tai Chi is a constant ebb and flow between Yang (preparation) and Yin (sinking or flow). When we are "on our way to the next movement," and move limbs, hands and feet to get in position, often breathing in as we do – that is a Yang action. Then as we exhale and sink and surrender into the form, onto our filling leg/foot and sinking onto the Vertical Axis and down, rooting into the Earth below, through the filling leg and allowing the flow to move out through our upper body as a push, punch, or whatever – this is the Yin non-action. The letting go, *the sinking*. We *let* the movement flow through us.

I know that some Tai Chi teaching thinks of a "punch" or a "push" as Yang, and I am not saying they are wrong. There is a Yang action quality to those types of actions. This is not about wrong or right. There are many facets of Tai Chi, like a vast diamond with so many facets that we can lose ourselves in their complexity.

But within each Yang action, like a punch, by allowing the Yin to take over (not thinking of forcing our punch, or forcing our body forward into the leg we are sinking into), but rather as we exhale on the punch, letting our entire being go and allowing the power of the punch to flow "through us," as we relax out of the way of it—allows the punch to be harder. When we are relaxed punches are faster and harder when thrown in real time. So we train in Tai Chi in slow time, in deep relaxation as the punch flows through us.

Also, we generally exhale when we punch or push. An exhale is the deepest way a human being can "let go." Letting go is a repose, or Yin experience. A human sigh or yawn (not the buildup of the in breath, but the great expending expression of a sigh or yawn in the dramatic exhale) is designed to unload energy when we get overwrought. That is why we sigh, to let go of energy overloads. Sighs are our primordial Qigong.

So, to recap, if your Tai Chi education thought of a punch or a push as Yang, they are correct, in that the action of a move is considered Yang. But, within every Yang quality in the universe, there is a Yin aspect as well. If we can allow that Yin, the letting go, to unleash through our push/punches and the like. the body becomes lax, like the Unbendable Arm. And the power of that punch comes not from us, but through engineering principles, from the earth beneath us, through our relaxed body and out through our hands or fist.

When I first began training in Tai Chi, I also trained in hard martial arts, and at first tried to "muscle" my punches. This was because our Yang world would have us think that this is what makes a punch powerful. Until I trained with Fumio Demura (at the time the only man to have won the world karate championship twice). Then I realized that you do not want to "muscle through" your punches, but rather surrender to them, which is Yin. You know who Fumio Demura is even though you may not realize it. When you saw the actor Pat Morita's character, Mr. Miyagi, fight in the shadows in the film "The Karate Kid," it was actually Fumio Demura who was doing the fighting in those scenes.

In karate, when you punch, you exhale loudly and deeply from your gut. It is called a "Kiai." It is partly to frighten your opponent, and partly to help the Qi, or Ki, explode from you when you strike. At that time as a younger man, I studied in several styles of karate, and found that there was karate, and then there was *karate*. Like Daniel-san in the Karate Kid, I experienced the Cobra-Kai-esque instructor (who reportedly had been kicked off a police force for brutality). And I also enjoyed the pleasure of a Mr. Miyagi-type teacher, which is how I think of Fumio Demura.

Each karate school or style had very different ways to "Kiai." Some with a "forced" exhale that sounded and felt tight and constipated. But Sensei Fumio's Kiai was explosive. Your entire being surrendered open to it and a force exploded out of you as you relaxed out of the way, and let it flow through you like a firehose unleashed.

Fumio Demura often reminded us that the power of the punch is not in the "muscles," but rather in the relaxation within you, that allows the punch to pour through you unimpeded. This surrender is the ultimate Yin act.

I began to realize that the same was true in Tai Chi, but at an even deeper level. When we exhale into a punch and "sink" into the leg, we are advancing into as we punch, that is an act of "absolute letting go." This Yin release is what allows the Unbendable Arm effect to go through our entire body. It lets the power of the planet earth flow through our relaxed body and out through our fist as we exhale.

Bruce Lee wrote that true power is found in absolute relaxation. This is the essence of Tai Chi—not the muscling things through, but the "absolute surrender of our being," even as we go through the motions of our lives.

In our first years of Tai Chi, our mind is filled with the Yang. Partly because in the back of our mind we are always in a hurry to get into the next movement, for fear that we may not remember how to get there if we wait too long. Also partly because our balance isn't as good as it will be in the future. So we rush movements to avoid teetering off our balance.

But in time, we grow more comfortable with our movements and our balance, and our breathing becomes our movements. Often in-breath Yang; in preparation, and exhale Yin; surrendering to the flow, to gravity, sinking into legs and forms.

In time the focus becomes not Yang body movements, where feet, arms, and hands are moving. Rather the focus becomes more and more on the subtle intangible. An almost invisible "sinking" deeply into the leg we are filling, and deeply surrendering to the power or flow washing through our effortless form and body, as we punch, push, and move. We become an empty vessel for our form to flow through.

We are no longer the source of our power. We are humble and without desire, without intent or destination. In that humility and desire-lessness the power of the universe has space to flow through us, as we are flowed through our Tai Chi forms. Tai Chi is about becoming unhinged, becoming flow, no destination/expectation, riding waves of flowing possibility whose breadth, depth, and width is beyond anything we could ever imagine, for we are lost in the Yin mind, lost in *the flow*.

The Yang mind thinks, "I must hurry up to my next Tai Chi movement while I still hold it in my mind." The Yin mind, as we flow through our Tai Chi movements, thinks, "Where am I?" I got this line from one of my advanced Tai Chi students and now a teaching assistant, a fascinating man named Kurt. Kurt is an engineer. Kurt's line described well about doing Tai Chi in the Yin mind, as we flow through the forms and the mind no longer thinks about hurrying up to get things done, but asks, "Where am I?" Lost in the flow.

I first taught Tai Chi and Qigong Meditation to engineers en masse when I was commissioned to teach these Internal Arts for Stress Management, at a huge international engineering company called Black & Veatch. That was a challenge for me, because I would get questions I had never gotten before, such as, "Why is the Vertical Axis 25 feet?" These are things no one asked when I studied Tai Chi, we just accepted these concepts. So it was trying for me as a teacher at first.

It was trying because I was there to help them "let go" of their Yang mind. As I was guiding them through Nei Gong Meditations, building a paradigm step-by-step with the breath work and the imagery designed to get them to "let go," and unhinge from left brain thinking, many of them were considering the engineering aspects of this Yin nebulous world. A world I was trying to get them to surrender and freefall into. I'm sure you can see how this was challenging for me.

But what I began to appreciate was the beauty of their Yang mind and Yang ways as they began to experience this Yin world. A world that was so strange and intangible to many of them when we began, even more than it was for me. Tai Chi and Qigong Meditation and Taoist concepts stretched them in ways, even beyond the ways it stretched this small town Kansas boy 40 years ago.

Yet as they transitioned these worlds, they had insights that they could put into words in ways that I never could, like my advanced student, Kurt. He realized one day that his Yang mind of keeping track of his Tai Chi forms, and hurrying to the next one to be efficient, fell away at some point. And then his Yang mind was no longer in charge keeping track of things. His Yin mind was lost in flow, and its only question, if it spoke in words, would be, "Where am I?"

There is nothing more beautiful than when the Yin and the Yang worlds intersect. This is where new paradigms emerge from. This world will transform in huge ways as we, as a society, embrace the Internal

Meditative Arts, and allow the endless and depthless creativity of the Yin to find its way into the society we are creating in the Yang world.

It will be a more expansive world, more connected and holistic, more compassionate and effective. A new order will emerge from the old, just as it happens on the microcosmic scale in our own lives, as Tai Chi and Qigong Meditation and Internal Arts practitioners. As we see our mind, our body, our heart become larger and more adaptable, and see our whole approach to life improve in so many ways, some apparent, and some nebulous and intangible. It is the Taoist way, the Tai Chi way, and in our modern world it is the *necessary way*. For in a world of ten billion people, humanity simply must learn to let go of old ways and adapt to new demands.

Just as Bruce Lee saw that the ultimate power came from absolute relaxation and letting go, Albert Einstein saw that ultimate creativity came from letting go, as his greatest insights came to him in moments of meditative drifting, and just as the great Indian mathematician, Srinivasa Ramanujan saw his elegant world altering theorems lilt into his mind during meditation – Yin receptive consciousness.

Creativity, dramatically expanded creativity, is an absolute necessity for humanity to handle the torrential change rushing at us faster and faster.

Timelessness

The Yin mind says, "Where am I?"

When students learn the long form of Tai Chi, they are still operating in the Yang mind for a while. Even when the beginning movements are now beginning to feel more Yin, having been performed so many times that they flow more effortlessly and naturally. But the final section of the movements are still new enough to keep the mind operating in Yang, especially if you are studying a Long Form.

In time, advanced students who have been doing the long form for a long time will reach a moment where they know they have shifted from Yang Mind to Yin Mind Tai Chi. It is when they no longer have the feeling that 'It will take a long time to get to the end of the long form.' Suddenly, they realize when they get near the end of the long form, 'Hey, I'm nearly at the end! This can't be right! What movements did I leave out, this went too fast?' Even as your movements are often actually slowing down as you get more proficient at them. Your breaths become deeper, longer, and slower. Your movements, wedding to your breaths, become slower as you sink deeper into each movement, and feel the sinking throughout your being in deeper and deeper ways. But again, even as our Tai Chi slows down in clock time, meaning that it should feel as though our form takes longer, our Long Form goes by in the blink of an eye. This happens when our mind loses itself to the Yin experience, almost as if we have gone through a Worm Hole that enables one to traverse universes, by folding the universe upon itself.

When we move into the Yin Mind, time is different, we move into another paradigm. Why does this happen? Again, in the beginning, before our Tai Chi movements become secure in us, become a part of us, we tend to always be hurrying to the next move. As if we are afraid we may forget what comes next if we don't hurry. Also, our balance is not as good as it becomes later, which causes us to rush into movements, because we fear losing our balance.

As we become one with our movements over time, integrating breathing with each movement (and our balance gets better and better), things slow down as we focus. Not on the Yang moves and transitions, but rather on the sinking, the surrender into each movement. In this state there is no destination. We are always flowing from one posture to another. A seamless flow, no beginning or end. This is the rhythm of life, always on our way toward something else. Nothing in the universe is static, and the belief that anything is, is a delusion. We are totally immersed in that present, of change and flow.

When we let go of the idea we always need to be somewhere else all the time, and we stand in the center of where we are, we are in the center of the universe. There is nowhere to rush to. Here, the universe comes to us. The world seems still as we stand in the center of it. Time no longer drives us like a slave master cracking his whip. We become surfers on time and space, riding currents of energy toward the future unfolding before us.

As I mentioned before, Lao Tzu explained that in this moment it feels as though we are doing nothing. But at this point, this moment, is when everything we need to do is being done. When we enjoy the beauty of our Tai Chi or Qigong motions, soaking into the pleasure of it, all the health benefits come to us. Even as it seems like we are doing nothing at all.

What I have found to be fascinating is that this quality of doing the most, when it feels like doing nothing, ripples far beyond our Tai Chi experience, and out into the fabric of our lives. It is as though the Tai Chi experience were a microcosmic portal through which we can experience our entire lives.

This Ch'an or Zen quality that Tai Chi play hones in us, that sense of being absorbed in, immersed in, lost in the moment even as we flow through changes, becomes part of our work, our relationships and our life. As I progressed in Tai Chi, conversations I had with my children changed. I was more present, more *with* the experience. This was true of my relationships with others.

When we skim the surface of life, everything is tedious because we are always impatiently waiting for this event, this conversation, this moment to end, so we can move on to the next one. Which seems so important until we get to it, and then it also becomes tediously in the way of the next thing we are rushing to.

But, when we let ourselves *sink* into the center of a conversation, an experience, it becomes depthless – sacred.

Each moment is sacred, until we feel an urgent need to move on. And then at that instant nothing is sacred. Only this moment, right now, at any given moment is sacred. When we stand in the center of it, everything is sacred, and a timelessness occurs.

When we are in those moments we feel connected to everything, so there is nowhere to rush to. Taoism tells us that the universe exists within us, that we touch the entire universe when we turn within. What is fascinating to learn so many decades after I first read this Taoist concept, is that modern physics is now telling us much the same thing. Einstein called it the "spooky effect," and physicists do not understand what is actually happening. But it appears that every particle in the universe may be somehow connected to every other particle in the universe.

We, it turns out, are what physics was about. Not some intangible "out there" thing in a sterile laboratory somewhere, but "right here," and "right inside us," "right now," at each moment.

You Are Energy

To flow with Tai Chi in the ultimate way, we must un-grip ourselves from the delusions we squeeze so tightly, so that we can open to the sweet flowing ocean of reality waiting to flow through us. This energetic nature of our being is a reality that can be very helpful to the Tai Chi player, so let's explore it.

We think of ourselves as solid beings, separated from the universe. This is a myth according to Albert Einstein, one of our greatest Western scientific minds. In fact, we are connected to everything. How is this possible? To understand how we are connected to everything, we must first understand what we are.

We must first understand that we are "made of energy." That is all we are when you look at the little bits that make us up. "Just energy," and in fact, we are mostly empty space in a field of "potential energy."

It is worth reiterating here what I learned of our physical make up at the Noetic Sciences conference, and was confirmed in the TV series, Cosmos, with Neil deGrass Tyson. For this sets us up to truly open to our energetic nature as a reality, and not just Taoist mystical poetry.

If you could take an atom out of any part of the universe, say out of your own body, and somehow blow it up to be big enough to see, the nucleus of that atom would be the size of a BB in the center of an American football field. The electrons going around it would be the size of dust motes 50 yards away in the end zone. This is so different than the image many of us were raised with in school, where models of atoms were a big blue ball (the nucleus) connected by Tinker Toy-type sticks to orange balls (electrons). We had the mistaken idea that the universe was made out of these big clunky balls of matter.

The reality is that, as you see in the BB and dust mote model above, we are mostly "empty space," or more accurately "potential energy field." In fact, even the BB and dust mote, or the particles we are, are only energy waves. There is no solid mass. But, even if you considered the BB and dust motes, or particles, as solid mass, they are such a tiny part of our being. To truly understand just how light and airy we are, consider this. If you could somehow get rid of all the empty space, or energy field, that we are made of, and you could somehow smush all of the sub-atomic particles together into one lump … the entire human race … the entirety of humanity … would only add up to one single grain of rice. Mind blowing, is it not? But, it is as true as the sun rising as the Earth turns each day.

When you think of this it feels as though the wind could blow right through you, and that is the mood most conducive to the Qigong and Tai Chi as Qigong experience. As we sigh out each breath, surrendering our grip on the idea that we are solid and separate, so that the Qi or life energy can flow through our loosening, opening being.

When we yield and surrender to this reality we realize that we are not a single solitary entity divided from the universe, but rather a rising wave from the ocean of energy that is all existence. The Yin Yang, or Tai Chi symbol, contains black and white dots in the 2 waves. Those dots are smaller Yin Yang symbols, and within those dots are smaller ones, and on and on. Ancient Chinese mystics were trying to explain the "self-replicating nature of the universe" that modern Chaos Mathematicians are now beginning to understand. Our state as energy beings, emerging from a field of potential energy of the universe, is originally seen in the smallest image of the sub-atomic particle. A particle emerging from the quantum field, from which all things emerge from. We are part of the endless ocean of energy, the quantum field from whence all things in the universe emerge.

As particles emerge from the quantum field, we are energy waves emerging from the energy of the universe. For we, our being, is the macrocosm of the microcosm of quantum particles.

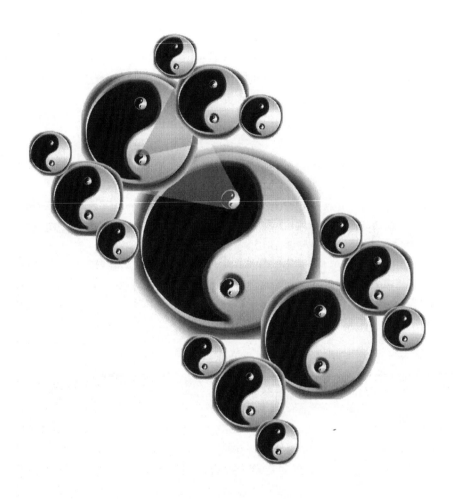

The Field

Tai Chi can become Qigong when "the breath" becomes part of the movements. It is at that point that the Yin mind, the surrender, the yielding and flow, can take us as we let go of control. This Yin state of mind takes us into the meditative state, where we open to the flow of life energy and become aware of our own energetic nature.

The word "Qigong," directly translated from Chinese, has 2 meanings: one is, "breathing exercise," and the other is "life energy exercise." The word "spirit" is from the Latin root "spiritus," which means "breathing," or "the breath." On opposite sides of the planet, the ancients understood that our ethereal or energetic nature was connected with "the breath."

As we move through the world, we see ourselves as separate beings, but this is illusion. We are manifest waves of energy in an endless ocean of energy. The entire universe is energy, as are we. This is not

Chinese mystical wonderings, but hard modern quantum physics. It is undeniable fact, and anyone holding onto the myth that they are solid separate beings, unconnected from the world and universe around them are squeezing onto a delusion. When we squeeze onto delusions, it tightens the mind, the heart, the field that we are, the tissue of our being. And our Tai Chi forms cannot flow unimpeded through us, like the airy cosmic winds of Qi flowing through our movements. We must let go of illusion to reach the highest state of Tai Chi, the state of flow.

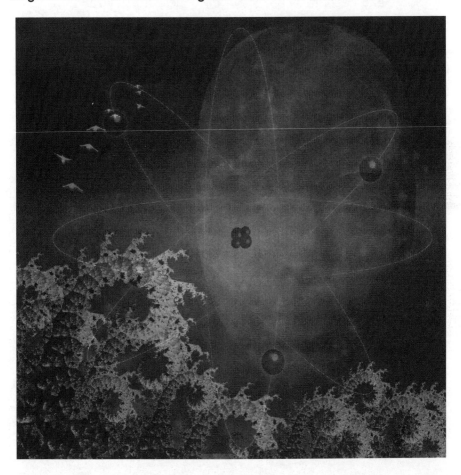

In Hindu mythology a prominent figure is Shiva, the Destroyer. In the West we think of the destroyer as a bad thing, but this is not what Shiva represents. Shiva represents the constant birth and formation of waves of energy that we call things and beings, which then eventually recede back into "the field" from whence all things spring. Lao Tzu called it the "Tao," the "way of the universe." Quantum physicists describe the "quantum field," the field of potential energy that all particles (which make up every single thing in the universe, including you and me), emerge from. The quantum field, the foundation of all things, is a constant dance of birth and death (Shiva's dance if you will) where particles emerge from the quantum field, and become manifest reality that can be observed in a physical way. Before again receding back into the quantum field. Like the particles, we, our existence, is a manifest wave of energy that will one day again recede back into the field. But we can also recede into this field of larger reality in ways when we surrender into the Yin state, the meditative state, where one loses one's sense of self and recedes into the field.

When doing Tai Chi forms, the Yin mind says,

"Where am I?"

Fritjof Capra was a physicist who had an ethereal experience that changed him and his view of the world forever. He then spent his life trying to reconcile his Yang analytical background of physics with his newfound spirituality. The fruits of his journey produced pearls of wonder and wisdom exploring our energetic nature, and the energetic nature of our universe, including a groundbreaking book entitled, "The Tao of Physics."

"The Tao of Physics" contains quotes from ancient mind-body meditative mystics as well as cutting edge quantum physicists. As you progress through the book you become incapable of determining whether a given quote came from a mystic or a physicist, because their understanding of the energetic nature of reality is so completely synonymous.

My life, my Tai Chi journey, has been one of trying to understand, trying to make sense of what I have experienced. Could this "field" reality of the universe, where everything is connected, explain how a being could have come to me as a boy of 6 years old, and given me a pre-lesson. Preparing me for what would happen to me many years in the future? Could this explain how a Taoist monk could foresee what I would do with my life a decade later? Could it explain how my sister in Kansas could have known what I was writing in California at the time? Or could it even explain how my deceased mother could have seen what I was doing after her death, and sent me a message of encouragement to keep me on a path that would eventually affect the world?

I warned you at the beginning of this book, that this *Tao of Tai Chi* journey, which led to this book, could not be surgically removed from "my story." So bear with me.

My Taoist journey has not been one of picking up a book to memorize the words and get some book-smarts. I have been a seeker, trying to make sense of a life, and life experiences, that could not be explained with the words and definitions I had been given in school.

And although my Tai Chi journey began from a need to handle the stress of life, when joined with Taoist philosophy, my Tai Chi journey became a journey of discovery that stretched from deep within, outward to the farthest reaches of the universe and beyond. As I surrender to this larger life and world, one can only ask:

"Where am I?"

The Spirituality of Tai Chi (not religion, but an ecumenical spirituality open to all beings, all faiths, to those with no religion, anyone and everywhere).

In order to do Tai Chi at its highest level, it requires us to "let go" of all things. To let go of "grudges," "fears," to let go of "desires."

Why is that? Because these gripping concepts constrict our mind, heart and physical tissue. The smooth unimpeded flow of Qi or life energy cannot expand or flow through us and through our Tai Chi movements as powerfully as they can when we "let go."

And as we let go again and again in Tai Chi, we begin to understand that all the things we hold against others are actually constricting and harming "us."

Forgiveness then becomes a profound all-encompassing experience, not some tight dogmatic mental effort we have to bestow upon others, as if we are doing them a great favor. It becomes something required of us to do if we want to become open vessels. So that the Qi and life force and our Tai Chi movements can flow through unrestricted and *unimpeded* by the tight-grippy thoughts we often squeeze within us.

Some Chinese masters call Tai Chi and Qigong a "return to child-likeness." Children's greatest asset is their ability to be in constant wonder, continually letting go of all they hold onto, to be completely in the moment of newness unfolding through them. To behold each moment with new eyes of wonder. Research shows that this state is most conducive to learning and absorbing new information.

Einstein said that if we are not in a constant continual state of amazement, we are as good as dead. Tai Chi can, at its highest level, help us to continually let go of everything we grip in our lives, in order to allow the smooth unimpeded flow of motion to pour through us. When that happens all the world is new and fresh.

If I rush into a supermarket I am in a Yang state of mind. I am on a mission with a set of tasks I must perform, holding them, sometimes squeezing them in my heart and mind. However, when I sit in my car before entering the store and "breathe" and "let go," and fall into that Yin state where my mind lets go of mental control (and my knowing awareness allows the light of the universe, the lightness of the universe, to expand through it), then my spine and nervous system's sensory awareness lets go of trying to feel or trying not to feel. My heart, lungs, liquid and glandular system sigh and allow my emotional awareness to let go and open to the lightness of my energetic nature ... I no longer rush into the store with a mission.

I feel the cool air conditioner on my face as I walk through the doors of the supermarket. I see the extraordinary beauty of the egg-plant's purple majesty, succulent and massive in its glory. The golden yellow of bananas and peppers, the smells of fruits and flowers, the kaleidoscope of color. I see the precious flowing energetic beings like me flowing through this beauty. The music ripples through me from the store's sound system and the scene becomes a trip, a journey, a happening, rather than another drudgery and mission in my life.

I still get the things I need done, but it is a completely different reality now. As Lao Tzu told us, we are capable of getting all things done, even as it seems like we are doing nothing, when we take the time to breathe, to un-grip, and to flow in our Yin mind.

In this state, the other waves of universal energy, the other people we encounter, become sacred and connected to us, and conversations often come more easily. We feel less isolated in the world, less alone, part of the field from whence we all have emerged from. Even as we perform our tasks we may find magic in others, may find space for a kind word leaving another being *less alone* than before we arrived.

Often the rush of life is fear based. If we can breathe, and let go, and have faith that everything will be alright even if we don't squeeze control in our minds and hearts … there is room to breathe … to be … sacred moments become possible … connection, true connection with others becomes possible … the world becomes magical, beautiful, and without fear.

Seeing the Qi

My first trip to Hong Kong in 1981 would blow the barn doors off my idea of reality, and allow my mind to stampede on an open range that never would have been possible, without that first amazing trip to Hong Kong. Not to stretch metaphors too much, but when I look back it was like approaching one of those cosmic gates you see in science fiction films or Star Trek episodes, where it is not just a doorway they are traversing, but stepping into a whole new universe.

Before I went to Hong Kong in 1981 I spent months working hard to finish learning my Guang Ping Yang Style Long Form, because I wanted to impress my new mother-in-law with my 64 posture Long Form. What I would learn later was that the I Ching, the Chinese Book of Changes, used 64 trigrams to divine the future. I would have smirked at all of this, had the weight of it not hit me in the face like some gentle Taoist sledgehammer. It hit me in a way that would change everything – me, my life, and how I see the universe we live in.

In Hong Kong in 1981, I would learn that one day I was to become a teacher. It would not be my Tai Chi teacher who would tell me this was going to happen, it would be a perfect stranger, a Taoist monk in a famous Taoist Temple on the other side of the planet. And he would tell me a full decade before the thought would ever enter my mind in any real way (see next chapter).

I would long forget about this Taoist monk and his prediction of my life's work, because I never had any intention whatsoever to become a Tai Chi teacher in my first 10 years of study. I was just trying to heal. That was my only goal. It was years after I had become a teacher and had written my Tai Chi book, and spread Tai Chi awareness through society at all levels all around the planet, that my wife reminded me of the Monk's premonition at the Taoist Temple so long ago. I had barely memorized the Guang Ping Yang Style's 64 forms before going to Hong Kong, and my mother-in-law was not impressed with my amateurish forms. At that time, I doubted that I would even be able to memorize all the forms of my style of Tai Chi. The idea of teaching was not in the picture at all, which is why I forgot about it. But the moment my wife reminded me it was as clear as if it had happened yesterday. How strange, a Kansas boy who had grown up transfixed by the Temple scenes of Kwai Chang Caine's Taoist lessons in the Kung Fu series on TV, many years later being told by a Taoist Monk in a Temple in Hong Kong, what my life's work would be – years before it would happen – by consulting the Taoist Book of Changes, the I Ching.

But a teacher I became, and like I mentioned, teaching in rather vast and extraordinary ways. Teaching millions via interviews I've done with some of the world's largest media institutions, in countries all over the planet. And via my globally published book in several languages. My DVD, CD, web pages, via my articles and newsletters read by people all over the planet, and in classes I have taught personally all over the planet. Teaching in some of the world's largest medical networks, and for some of the world's largest corporations, prisons, and more.

Ask yourself, how the heck could a stranger on the other side of the planet have known that "I would become a teacher," when I had no idea of it myself, no plans for it, and then had lacked years of formal education that my society would demand of me to become "a teacher"? Tai Chi was only a pastime for me, a mental health practice to manage my stress, to heal from my past. Never in a million years did I think I would ever be a Tai Chi teacher in 1981. Yet here I am, my educational efforts known worldwide. How the heck was this possible?

My first introduction to the I Ching would be on this trip in 1981 in Hong Kong. When the Taoist monk in a famous Temple would tell me a fate that sounded so odd that I laughed in his face, and dismissed what he told me. I would later learn that the I Ching was connected to Taoist philosophy's seeing the world as an interconnected whole, a field of energy. That would mesmerize me because of my real life experience with a Taoist monk, who had divined my future using Taoist tools. I would wonder what it meant that my Tai Chi form contained 64 postures, and the Taoist I Ching book of divination used 64 trigrams to determine things like the monk determined, about my life's destiny and work.

Over the decades of my life I became fascinated by quantum physics, and how quantum field theory, and quantum non-local theory, might explain how a monk in Hong Kong could know a Kansas boy's life's future. And how a sister in Kansas could know that I was in California, with a stack of stories and poems I'd written after an angel had visited me. Or how an angel 55 years ago had known to prepare that Kansas boy to learn "Qigong" "breathing exercises." I began to see science as, not a religion that held all the answers to everything, but as what it really is. Which is an important and valuable attempt to explain the unexplained, which is an ongoing struggle. As our experience of reality expands, science has more to explain. In history there have always been those who think that what is currently accepted represents all there is to know. They have continually been proven wrong in the end, as technology and creativity have evolved, and we have learned that science can explain even more; from the Earth revolving around the sun and not the other way around, to the realization that atoms were not solid, but rather their particles were energy waves. And now Chaos mathematics is showing us that there is indeed order, in what we once thought of as indiscernible chaos. What was once thought to be beyond the realms of science and mathematics

Hong Kong's experience eventually drew me to quantum physics. But it wasn't just the I Ching and the Taoist monk's predictions. I also had an amazing personal experience in Hong Kong in 1981 – I SAW QI, an energetic nature of our being.

At that time Qi was considered a myth by science. But today we have studies from major research institutions showing both the effect of External Qi emitted from one person to another, and also detectable qualities of the Qi emission in measurable ways. In our lifetime science will reveal much more. I am certain because of my experience. Qi, life energy, opening to the flow of Qi, is at the heart of Tai Chi. The experience I had in Hong Kong drew me toward neurological and physical sciences. Not to be smarter, but to help me make sense of amazing events and experiences I had, even before taking that astounding trip to Hong Kong in 1981, where this concept of Qi was driven deep into my mind and life experience.

I do not think that to be one with the Tao, to experience the field, the Qi, one has to "see the Qi." I say this because I do not "see Qi" for the most part. Rather I feel it, or perhaps feel the results of it. However, I have seen glimpses of Qi at times in my life. For the most part my experience of Qi is tactile, more of a sensory experience than a visual experience. When I "let go" there is space for the lightness, the effortlessness, to expand and flow through. Or radiate through me, and I enjoy that sense of uncontrolled flow pouring through me like a silken spring breeze or an angel's ethereal caress. Kind of massaging the atoms of energy field of my being, as I relax out of the way and open to the flow or radiance that moves through and beneath and expands within all things, when we relax out of its way.

I have come to see Tai Chi and Qigong as not the source of Qi, but more accurately as powerful tools designed to loosen and shake off the tension dust. So that we can open to the lightness and effortlessness waiting to expand and flow through us, each time we "let go" of our grip on ourselves, on our lives, and on our world. The Qi, the life energy, is a radiance that is always expanding and radiating through us, only waiting for us to let go of our grip and allow space for it to shine through us. To be filled with Qi, shining with it, radiating it, which is our natural state. To experience that, can seem like a struggle, but it is actually the opposite of struggle and effort. What makes that seem so hard is the distortion we have built up in our minds, and in our lives and world, that everything has to be hard and difficult and effortful.

As I mentioned, I have seen Qi a few times in my life. The most frequent times I have seen it has been on rare occasions, when I was doing Tai Chi in my backyard or at the park in the springtime, when the world was calm and fresh and bursting with life. As I was doing Single Whip and my hand would pass just beyond my line of vision, as I exhaled and let go and sank into the completion of the movement, I would sometimes glimpse the shine coming off my fingertips.

I think that some animals and babies may have a propensity for seeing Qi. I once had a Pekinese dog who saw my Qi. She was a strange mean dog, who bit everyone in our family at one time or another. But when I did Tai Chi or Qigong meditation around her she would stare at me. And when I was done, she would lick the air an inch or so beyond my fingertips, as if my fingers were an inch longer than they were. She was trying to lick the energy she saw extending out from my fingertips. I think my granddaughter sees Qi as well. When I perform Tai Chi in front of her, at times it captivates her. At other times she loses interest. But when my Long Form is complete and my arms and hands raise up and over my head, and come down in the final movement of energetic downpour we call Grand Terminus in the Guang Pin Yang Style Long Form, she is always staring at me in wonder from her infant stroller seat, which she rides in to the park where I do Tai Chi. I have a video on Youtube you can look at. Just Google "Baby calmed by Tai Chi Youtube" and it should come to the top, and you can see how Tai Chi and Qigong mesmerized her for 40 minutes, when I first performed Tai Chi and Qigong in front of her when she was 5 months old.

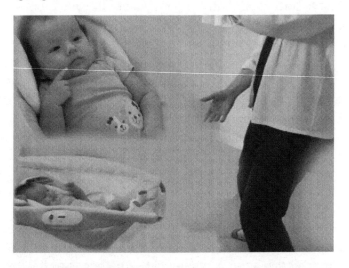

I know for a fact that it "is" possible to see Qi. Because, there was one occasion when I fully saw Qi emanating from people in a way that was just as clear as the chair I am now sitting on, or the computer I am now typing on. I remember that day as if it happened a few moments ago. I was in my early 20s, and had been practicing Tai Chi and Qigong for about a year. It was that life altering trip I had mentioned before, when my wife and I were newlyweds traveling to Hong Kong so I could meet her family. I had been studying my Guang Ping Yang Long Form very diligently for months, because I wanted to impress my mother-in-law with my Tai Chi form. I knew that she had practiced Tai Chi when my wife was a young girl in Hong Kong. When we got to Hong Kong, I suffered horrible jet lag. Having never flown internationally before, the jet lag hit me hard. When we first arrived, I fell asleep and slept through the feast my mother-in-law had prepared in our honor. No one could wake me up, I was out of it, and I slept for about 28 hours before waking up to be told what I had done.

Then, for about three weeks my sleep was way off kilter. I was falling asleep early each evening, only to awaken at about three a.m. each morning, while Hong Kong slept. My mother and father-in-law had a very unique house up on a huge hill, overlooking the grand canyon of skyscrapers that was the Causeway Bay district of Hong Kong, on Hong Kong Island. Few people in Hong Kong had gardens, as most lived in that sea of endless high-rise apartments and condos. But my in-laws had a garden around their hilltop home. They weren't rich, they had just settled here many years before Hong Kong expanded and rose up all around them. Their home was surrounded by lush jungle-like flora. When you were in their garden it felt like you were in a home surrounded by jungle, until you walked out the garden gate and then beyond the concrete steps leading down the hill. Then you saw the endless expanse of Hong Kong's valley of skyscrapers below you.

When I woke up at three a.m. each day, as everyone in the house and most of Hong Kong slept, I went out into the garden and meditated and played Qigong and Tai Chi. I had never, and have never practiced these arts as intensely as I did at that time, because there was nothing else to do at 3 am. I meditated for an hour or two, and did Universal Post/Gathering Qi/Standing Post for long periods, eventually building up until I could Stand Post for about 45 minutes (a record for me).

After doing this for weeks, one day my wife and I were down at the docks waiting for a ferry boat to take us across the bay to the mainland, the Kowloon side of Hong Kong. It was a gray day and the water and the sky were about the same color, and it was early morning. We sat waiting, and I closed my eyes to meditate for a few minutes. When I opened my eyes the *most amazing sight* filled my eyes with wonder. A person walked by and I could see a plume of silvery shiny light emanating from the top of the person's head. And then another person walked by and I saw the same thing, and then another and another. There are energy points in the top of the head and just above the head, that we open to when doing Nei Gong, or energy work. I didn't see these points specifically, but like I said, I saw a plume of silvery light emanating from the top of the heads and trailing along with them as they walked by.

Then, I looked around the wharf and saw this phenomenon on every single person there. I was awestruck, and I nudged my wife, saying, "Do you see this?" She didn't. She had been sleeping like a baby every night in her childhood bedroom that we slept in, while I had been spending hours in the garden every day cultivating my Internal Arts.

After several minutes of watching this, this amazing phenomenon began to seem almost commonplace. I felt as though I would be able to see this forever. It was not to be, but I did see it for those 45 minutes or so as we sat on that dock. Then the ferry arrived and we boarded, and the sun came out from behind the clouds as we steamed off toward Kowloon Island, and I no longer saw the energy.

But that morning, during that time I had seen Qi so clearly for so long, the site of it had become so familiar that I was no longer completely gob-smacked by it. I had then begun to notice differences in the people's auras or energy plumes.

I noticed that the businessmen whose hands gripped their briefcases and minds seemed to be somewhere else, perhaps rehearsing lines for a meeting or something – had very small, tight, constricted energy plumes coming off their heads. However, the people that were completely "in the moment," chatting with friends or enjoying the view and the day, had huge shiny silvery plumes extending or radiating off of them. They shined with light. That realization stuck with me and affected my teaching and my study for my entire life. After that, when I studied Alan Watt's "The Way of Zen," and his other books and videos, it was not an intellectual experience anymore. It was something more real and deeper. I understood on a visceral level what "being in the moment" meant, how it affected our lives, and our connection with the energy field.

Zen is a Japanese phrase born of the Chinese word *Chán*, which means "just sitting." It means "being in the moment," here and now, feeling and sensing whatever comes into and through our awareness. Not hanging onto things or engaging things, but simple being there, witnessing their passage with no attachment. Suzuki, an Aikido master

(Aikido means "the path of Qi, spirit, or energy"), said in describing the state of meditation that 'we should keep the front door and back door of the mind open, and things will pass through, we just should not ask them to stop and have tea.'

Tai Chi is a vehicle for being completely in the ever evolving moment. Brilliant in its construction, for it is complex enough to keep the mind from worrying about our credit card debt, or whether we locked the door when we left home. But in time its forms become familiar enough so that we do not have to think about what comes next. We just allow the movements to flow us, and we are always in transition from one movement to the next. Never "in one movement, never pondering it," but rather flowing into change and transition, unimpeded, disentangled. This is the way of the Tao, of Qi, of spirit and energy.

Will I see Qi again one day? Perhaps, although my Tai Chi and Qigong practice has never been as intense and dedicated as it was at that special time in Hong Kong. And perhaps being in such newness, unencumbered by the world I was used to, drifting in a culture where I had not social familiarity, contributed to that gift of sight I was given that day. I would learn later in my studies that Zen Koans, such as "What is the sound of one hand clapping?" were riddles with no answer. Their purpose was to stun the mind, take it out of its normal thought patterns, where a newness of consciousness could have space to come through. Perhaps this initial Hong Kong journey, being so far from my normal routines and thought patterns, had been every bit as much a part of my Qigong and Taoist education as the angel coming to teach me Qigong as a child, or the other events leading to where I am now. Perhaps that entire trip; from the jet lag forcing me to do Tai Chi and Qigong for hours, to the Taoist monk, to the seeing Qi, to being thrown into another culture with entirely new ways of seeing the world, were a Zen Koan my Taoist journey had given me. Perhaps it does not matter if I ever see Qi again in that way. It may be that the purpose of that trip – all those strange events – was to open my mind and to shift my consciousness. Perhaps your picking up this book was part of *your* Taoist journey, to shift your consciousness. The Tao flows and swirls in ways beyond what we can fully comprehend, even at moments when it is changing everything, in every way, forever.

I will never be sure what factors contributed to it, or allowed it to happen. I only know that it changed me, changed my Tai Chi, and eventually influenced my teaching and writing about Tai Chi that has affected people worldwide through my Tai Chi book (published worldwide in several languages). And more importantly, it changed my life and the way I see the world, and my place in it.

That first trip to the East, to Hong Kong, rattled the foundations of who I am, and how I saw the world on many levels. I will share an extraordinary experience I had on that trip in the next chapter. And if you believe what I tell you, it may very well rattle you, and be a Zen Koan, a consciousness altering paradigm shifting experience, for you as well.

Just in case it may help for it to be so, I will assure you once again that everything I tell you in this book is absolutely true, and absolutely happened in real life, no matter how unbelievable it may seem when you read it.

There are More Things in Heaven and Earth
than are Dreamt of in Your Philosophy, Horatio

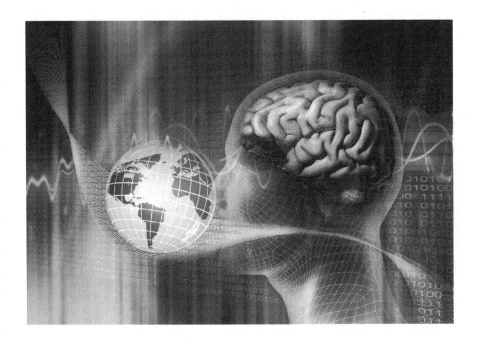

Previously, I briefly alluded to the event with a Taoist monk in Hong Kong, who propelled me to look deeper into Taoism. Here's more on how that fateful event unfolded.

On that first trip to Hong Kong, my brother-in-law Sammie Wong offered to take us to a famous Temple, famous for its fortune telling Taoist monks who could read the I Ching divination sticks, called Yarrow Stalks. I had never heard of this. And I had maybe only heard of the I Ching, the Book of Changes, in passing prior to that. I was anxious to give it a go, even while doubting anything would really come of it.

My wife and I entered the large Temple, which was a fascinating experience for a Kansas Lutheran boy, because the Temple was a social place, so different from my experience with churches. People were having picnic lunches around it, kids were running around and playing, while others knelt and lit incense and prayed and meditated all around us.

We walked to the center of the Temple where a large Buddha stood. Meeting my wife's family was a big eye opener for me, as a Lutheran boy from Kansas where religions were often segregated and held in mild or not so mild suspicion. The town that I grew up in was somewhat segregated back then. The Catholics lived on the North Hill, the north side of town, north of Highway 40, and the Protestants mostly on the South Hill and surrounding area. I remember my grandmother, a Christian fundamentalist, going to mass with my sister's family who were Catholics (her husband being Catholic). As I tried to follow the Catholics in their kneeling on the kneeling pad, and standing, and chanting, I noticed Grandma sat respectfully in silence, but not participating because her church said that Catholics were not real Christians. My new family in Hong Kong was way different than that. They were Catholics. My wife went to a Chinese Catholic school growing up, yet they had Buddhist and Chinese ancestor worship statues and things all around their house, and never saw any conflict between any of it.

So I followed my wife to the large statue of Buddha in the center of the Temple and followed her lead, taking the requisite number of Yarrow Stalks from the cup. And then placing them in our individual cups, and kneeling before the statue and contemplating questions we had, about ourselves or our lives, as we shook the cups until the requisite number of sticks fell out. Then I followed her to the monks in the tents outside the Temple, who we handed our Yarrow Stalks. They looked at them, retrieving large ancient looking scrolls and books, and then proceeded to tell us our fortunes.

My wife went first as I watched. I don't remember all that he told her that day, except I do remember the first thing he told after looking at her Yarrow Stalks, and pulling out the related scrolls and text. He said, "You are pregnant."

We both laughed at that, my wife first, and then me when she translated what he had told her in Cantonese. Because we both knew full well that my wife was NOT pregnant. 2 days later, while shopping on the steamy hot sweltering streets of Hong Kong, my wife grew ill and we went to a medical doctor. She drew blood from her, took it to the lab for testing, and came back into the room later to tell my wife, "You are pregnant." The monk was two days ahead of medical science!

Days before at the Temple, after my wife's Yarrow Stalks reading, the monk took mine. I don't remember all he said those many years ago, but what we do both remember is that he said that one day I would be "a teacher." We both laughed at that as well, because I had not even completed my bachelor's degree. I had dropped out of university when my wife had graduated, a year or so before I would have graduated, so we could move to California. My wife had come home after getting her degree and said, "I have to leave western Kansas and go somewhere where I can eat real Chinese food." So I dropped out of school and we moved just south of Los Angeles, where I would eventually start learning Tai Chi, because the stress of urban life had nearly driven that small town Kansas boy out of his mind, with 16 lane freeway traffic and the urban rat race. I had no designs to "teach Tai Chi."

Even though I had begun studying Tai Chi before we went to Hong Kong, I had zero intention of even pondering the idea of becoming a teacher. This was because my own Tai Chi teacher, Jais Booth, lived a few miles from me, and I just assumed that anyone wanting to learn Tai Chi would study with her, I was struggling just to remember my Tai Chi forms. So the monk's serious declaration that I would "be a teacher" seemed ridiculous that day. Of course now looking back, after having taught Tai Chi for 25 years, and writing 4 editions of globally published multi-lingual Tai Chi books, that have taught Tai Chi to people all over the world – we no longer are laughing at that monk's outlandish predictions. Just as we were no longer laughing at them two days after the monk had told my wife "she was pregnant," when the doctor walked in in her white lab coat with my wife's blood test results, saying, "You are pregnant."

Events like this begin to show you that there are 'more things in heaven and earth than are dreamt of in your philosophy.' It set the stage for me to find some humility in my certainty about life in the ensuing 40 years of life experience that would follow.

Perhaps this event opened my mind and heart to wisdom like the Tao te Ching, and to Tai Chi and Qigong concepts and philosophy that I would have closed my mind to, had this strange series of events not happened.

I was told a story once about a scholar who went to a Taoist master to study Taoism, because the scholar had wanted to add a "Taoist Study Degree" to his wall full of degrees. According to the story, the Taoist master greeted the scholar at his door and then offered him tea. When pouring the scholar's tea the Taoist master overfilled his cup, until it was spilling over the cup's brim, spilling across the table. Until the scholar exclaimed, "The cup is full already." The Taoist master explained, "Yes, just as you are too full of knowledge. There is no space left for me to share anything with you."

Humbling experiences like those I had on that first trip to Hong Kong, as a young American who suffered from the delusion that western science and American culture were the end-all-and-be-all of wisdom in the world, were perhaps the prerequisite for me to become the student of Tai Chi, Qigong, Taoism, and mind-body meditative practices and philosophies around the world, that I would become in the ensuing decades of my life. And prerequisite for my future world travels as World Tai Chi Day founder, always seeking and opening to new information. I was trying to understand the world and how it worked.

I had always been like that in a way, I suppose – a seeker. When I graduated from high school a man walked up to my mother and father. I learned that he had been my Sunday school teacher at the Lutheran church we'd attended when I was young. He told my parents that I had been his most difficult student in all his years of teaching Sunday school. When he saw the concern on my parent's faces, he clarified, "Oh, Junior wasn't disruptive. It was just that he was always asking questions that I did not have the answers to."

Hong Kong broke open that young Kansas man's mind, and in that opening expanded the questions that would surface through the ensuing decades, some of which I articulate in this book. Many of the answers I would find were that *there are not always answers* to everything. And that too was liberating and expanding.

Knowing that *all cannot be understood* is the purpose of Zen Koans, and it liberates us to behold and be amazed by things larger than we can comprehend at any given moment.

Tai Chi is a model for this. There are no answers in Tai Chi, there is only ongoing flowing amazement at the sensations and experiences flowing through us as we unhinge from what we are – and let the Tai Chi unfold us.

Experiencing the Field

When I was a small boy, after my angelic experience between the church and my Sunday school, I remember having other experiences that would only find context 15 years later, when I walked out of my first Tai Chi and Qigong Meditation class.

As a boy, I remember standing in the ripe wheat fields not far from my western Kansas home. I remember the warm summer wind humming through the wheat stalks and heads as I stood alone, away from the things of man. In the vibration of that drone of the wind strumming the wheat fields, for moments I would lose myself in that experience. Something would shift, and it felt strange and wonderful, as if a portal had opened to something huge and vast. Of course at that age I had no words for it. Even today, after having been a professional writer for nearly 20 years, I still lack words to fully describe it. But I think Lao Tzu and others have provided words that give us a glimpse of this field awareness, when we lose ourselves and merge with the field, the Tao, the underlying grid of the universe – the quantum field, perhaps.

Nearly 20 years after my experiences in the Kansas wheat fields, or when gazing up at the endless Kansas heavens, its towering pure white clouds and heartbreakingly beautiful blue sky, when I would "merge with the field" for moments, I had an incredible experience that brought the Tao te Ching to life for me in a way that has changed everything forever. My Tai Chi and Qigong practice, the way I teach it, and how I have played my own small role in spreading these tools more widely around the world. And in helping them gain acceptance in institutions and government bodies worldwide.

As all stories are, it is complicated. It is not just a Tai Chi story. But I know for certain that without my Tai Chi and Qigong Meditation experiences, loosening and opening me in deep ways, I would likely have never been prepared to have this experience, let alone be able to conceptualize it. Or maybe even have been able to remember it and articulate it as I can today.

As often happens with a big breakthrough, although I don't believe it has to happen this way, it began with great tragedy. I had not had much experience with death. No one in my immediate family had died, and when my grandfather had died (the only person I had known up to that point who had passed away), there was a sense that the universe was in order. He had lived a full life and his departure was not so unexpected. Also, we lived far away from him. So the actual drama of his death had not really touched the boy I was at the time in a visceral way.

Then life woke me up with a sledgehammer, within the span of about 18 months. I visited my mother in the hospital one day, and was told by her surgeon the next morning, that she had passed away in surgery. A few month later while I was still reeling from that, my father passed away. And then a few months after that, my youngest son fell into a coma. He lay in a coma in a hospital bed for one long excruciating month, before he died as I held him in my arms, as the doctor turned off his life support.

My wife had spent every day with my son, Isaac, sitting next to his hospital bed talking to his small body, which was hooked up to tubes and machines that made him breathe breaths. My job was to take care of our other two young children at home. Which I did, but I became so despondent that my alcohol intake rose steadily over those long painful weeks. I became hard and jaded.

The night my wife called me to come to the hospital because Isaac had suffered another heart failure. I loaded the kids in the car and drove through the dark desolate night in silence. A nurse met us at the door and took the kids to a nursery. My wife was waiting in the hospital room, dark except for the light at the head of Isaac's bed. We were prepared for this, or as prepared as two young twenty something parents could be, whose brains and nerves were fried and exhausted beyond comprehension. We had discussed this after Isaac's heart had failed a few days before and the staff had revived him. We decided, or I decided, that if Isaac "gave us a sign" that it was time to let him go, that we would do so. My wife, Angela, would never have let go. It was beyond her ability to let this precious being go, who she had nurtured in her womb, in her precious body. Who had drank from her body and held her so tightly before falling into that coma. She was unable to decide, so I walked in with the guilt of knowing that I had prodded her into this moment. The doctors had too, but I was the one who was "able to let go."

I already had let go, it was the only way I could bear the situation after this long month. I had convinced myself that Isaac was not that body in the bed anymore. I was hardened, and when the doctor asked me if I wanted to hold Isaac while they turned off the machines, I replied coldly, "No."

Then a voice came into my head, that said that this moment would change the rest of my life, and I stopped the doctor before he flipped the switch. I sat in the chair as the nurse placed Isaac's limp body in my arms. The cold shining single light at the head of his bed could not illuminate the dark room, or the darkness all around us on that night.

Emotionless, I held Isaac, only wanting to get outside and have a cigarette and a beer. Then the doctor flipped the switch and the respirator hissed its last breath. Isaac's lungs released the air, and the waving lines on the monitor went flat ... and the earth stood still.

I had only experienced anything like that when I was a very, very young boy, playing with a slingshot I had gotten as a present. I was shooting rocks with it, aiming at but most often missing the petals of the flowers, the petunias my father planted around our modest Kansas home for summer. I saw a hummingbird, beautiful, shining with colors reflected off its tiny feathers, its shining wings humming on the summer air. I reared back, stretching the rubber bands attached to the slingshot, feeling the sharp pebble between my thumb and forefinger in the slingshot's cradle. Knowing I would miss with this shot as well. I let it fly and in that moment the air whizzed with fury, and that hummingbird's headless, lifeless body stood in the air before falling to the ground. Everything in the world stopped moving, stopped breathing. God looked down upon me with such absolute shock and disappointment that I wanted to shed my skin and tear my heart out of my body. I wanted to repent, repent, repent for this horrible unspeakable act I had committed on God's beautiful delicate harmless creature.

So I knew this feeling I had, as the life lifted out of Isaac's fragile tortured body, but this was worse. Oh my God, there was no relief, no thought of a cigarette or a beer, no thought. My heart broke open; ripping everything I was apart, never to be the same again. Isaac's soul passed through my body and broke me into ten billion pieces. Oh my God, oh my God, oh my God, I can't stand this! *I CANNOT STAND THIS!* I wept like an old woman, heaving sobs wracking my being. I wailed and tears poured.

When I finally got home, I opened a beer. And then another one, and another one, and this became my way of life for weeks. But, I didn't move to whiskey, because my other two children's tiny fragile faces looked up to me still. I wanted to numb, but I didn't self-destruct. At least not immediately, although this path would have killed me, given the shape of my damaged liver.

Then one day I had an epiphany, realizing I did not want to go out this way. I poured my beer down the drain, threw out my cigarettes, and put on jogging shoes and ran out the door. Running until my legs trembled, my lungs burned with fury, and I could run no more. I began doing this daily, but I was still shattered on so many levels.

One night, still bewildered and lost even though I had decided to live, I got down on my knees. Something I hadn't done since I was a child. I knelt on the floor and leaned on the bed as I folded my hands, and said, "Please, show me why I am here. I have to know why I am here." I asked this because I just couldn't comprehend at that time why. Why we, why I was here, nothing made any sense, after a year and a half of being hammered by bone crushing losses that had turned my world upside down in a massively disorienting way. To become an orphan, and then to suffer the most excruciatingly unnatural loss a human being can ever experience – the loss of your child – had turned the world into a mad kaleidoscope like a carnival house of mirrors.

After my plea made kneeling by my bed, my plea to 'know why I was here," I then crawled into bed and began meditating until I fell asleep. Suddenly, at 3 am, I was awake finding myself sitting on the end of my bed in the dark. And "a being" was in front of me. I could not see it, but I could *feel* it.

And it "communicated" to me. At that instant, I realized that it was the same being I had seen as a young child, as an angel who had come to me when I was 6 years old. Who had flown me to my church and Sunday school, and had given me my first Qigong lesson, my "breathing exercise."

There at the foot of my bed at 3 am that dark California night, it reached out and "touched" me in the center of my heart. My heart that Isaac had broken so widely open a few weeks before. And my heart exploded in light. It was fantastically beautiful – my heart expanded open and became this expanding light. Then the being touched me in the center of my brain. In Tai Chi training I had been trained in Nei Gong energy work, and learned that there are three main centers in Tai Chi training: the Lower Dan Tien in the upper pelvis; the Middle Dan Tien in the heart; and the Upper Dan Tien in the center of the brain. But I wasn't thinking of any of that at this moment, even though that training may have prepared me in some way for this. This experience happening to me now at this moment on that night so long ago.

My brain exploded in light, expanding outward, until my heart energy and mind energy became one. Expanding outward and upward until the light, until *I* filled the room. I had become the light. I, the light, expanded outward and upward until I saw the ceiling of our bedroom rushing at me. Then I passed through seeing the slats in the attic, and then the pine trees over our house were rushing at me. I could see down behind me, and watched my home get smaller, and then saw Huntington Beach where we lived at the time, shrinking below. Then California, the West Coast, the United States, the Americas, and then the Earth shrinking behind me. I looked around and saw the moon rushing past me, expanding toward the stars as I continued to swell. I had not left my home, or the Earth, it was all part of me, everything was part of me.

At that moment, as I saw the Earth, that beautiful precious blue pearl, that lonely orb floating so vulnerable in the vastness of space – as vulnerable and fragile as that butterfly I had destroyed as a boy with my mindless cruel slingshot, as vulnerable as Isaac's limp tortured body in my arms in the hospital weeks before. This orb was in my heart, part of my mind.

In that moment, I felt the sorrows, aching love, despair, worry and fear of a thousand, a million, the billions of people all over that fragile precious planet. And I felt their fragile hearts, and longing for love and for their loved ones, their children, their parents, their homes and communities and nations. There were no boundaries, no walls, nothing separated us ... we are all part of "the field," the energy of life that permeates every single thing in this universe.

My heart swelled like a dove lifted on a wind toward the swirling tidal skies, beautiful enough to break your heart. And my heart broke as human beings all over the world felt those they love slip away from them. The woes, the love, the preciousness of humanity broke me and opened me, and I would NEVER see the world the same again. National boundaries would never mean anything to me. Religions, race, and all the things that divide people would never have any meaning to me again, not as divisive things I mean.

Then suddenly I became afraid, afraid that I was dying. Perhaps this is what it feels like to die, I thought. And just as when I had become afraid, and lost my faith, and held my breath as a young boy when the angel had taught me to fly, I began to drop down. Everything that had expanded within, throughout and all around me, suddenly went into reverse, collapsing and descending, until I slammed back into my body like a giant vault door had slammed shut.

I was sitting on the end of my bed trembling, gasping for air. The last message this being had imparted to me when I lost faith, and the miracle I had experienced and collapsed back down, was, "Fear closes all doors. Fear closes all doors. Fear closes all doors."

On shaking legs I walked out of my dark bedroom and out into my kitchen, knowing there was no way I was going to be able to sleep. On the kitchen table was a pen and paper that "called to me." I sat down and began writing all the things flowing through my mind as fast as I could. I was not intellectually considering what I was writing, it was as if I was a stenographer taking dictation from all the images and feelings rushing through my being. This night was when I became a writer, years before I would actually sell anything I would write. And never intending to do so, just being driven to manifest the nebulous messages pouring through my mind, my being.

The first thing I wrote was a poem, and it took me years to realize what it was about. But I now know it wasn't about me, it was about the "being" who had visited me that night. But it was also about the "field" nature of reality. That angel's mission was to awaken us to that reality that "all things are connected." Just as Einstein tried to tell us, and spiritual leaders of all the major religions have tried to tell us. Here is the poem:

I have come to heal this world.

To show men what they already know.

To make the obvious apparent,

and drive common sense home

until the anvil of consciousness

splinters beneath the hammer of that sense.

And from that shattered anvil

a simple steely truth shall be forged,

that when one of us suffers ... *so do we all.*

I have come to realize over decades, that this "experience" was meant for many reasons. One was to let me experience "the field," the web of energetic existence that connects all of us to everything and everyone.

Nei Gong or Sitting Qigong Meditation can enable me to touch the edge of the hem of the garment of this extraordinary reality, giving me glimpses of what I felt, as for moments I come unhinged and freefall or free-float, losing myself in the field.

My regular meditation reminds me of this truth, this truth that all things are connected. A truth that quantum physicists are finding in nonlocality experiments. Remember that these experiments showed that subatomic particles over vast distances reacted simultaneously when one particle was affected, faster than the speed of light, Meaning that matter is somehow connected. It is as if existence were a huge endless sheet of paper that we see as reality, but when we lose ourselves and merge with the field, the universe is like that piece of paper rolled up into the tiniest most compact paper wad. Where all the pieces of paper are simultaneously touching one another. This is a crude analogy, but it gives an idea of what *nonlocality* and *field reality* mean.

After decades of Tai Chi practice, one begins to lose oneself in the flow, and it is very common for Tai Chi players to have a great sense of *connection* afterwards.

Modern neurological science is beginning to understand the impact of mind-body practices. Technology now allows neurologists to actually see inside the human body and mind. We know that Tai Chi literally makes the physical brain larger. Research on meditation proves that it can cause the part of the brain that makes us feel isolated to become less active, which can leave us feeling a greater sense of connection, and less isolated.

Another effect of meditation can be the actual shrinking of the fear part of the brain, and the enlargement of the empathy and compassion part of the brain. Some research shows that when meditators see images of people suffering, their brain's empathy/compassion center goes into reaction. And that the "action" part of the brain also fires up. Meaning that meditators are more prone to run to the aid of others, feeling stronger empathy driving them to action.

My own experience leads me to believe that when we meditate, when we practice mind-body meditative experiences (which I believe Tai Chi and Qigong can be if we wish to practice them as such), we lose ourselves when the brain drifts into Alpha wave brain vibratory states. At those moments we experience "the field." I believe that this field experience results in our brains experiencing us and our world differently than before, and that is what changes the physical brain. Some may believe it is the other way around. That meditation physically changes the brain, and this affects the way we see the world in a new way. But I see it as a larger perception of reality changing the brain.

Physics' nonlocality makes me believe that it is not just "a new way of thinking," but rather our opening to a higher reality. Physics shows us that reality is connected. Einstein emphatically made the point that it is a delusion that we think we are not connected to the universe.

Neurologists and pathologists have found that when pianists are autopsied, the nerves of their thumb and a finger that makes repetitive piano key strikes simultaneously, are wired together. Something that is not the case in non-pianists. This means that the experience they had over and over again is what changed their brain.

Therefore, again, I believe that when we "lose ourselves" in the Yin meditative flow of Tai Chi or Nei Gong meditation, we touch into the field. I think that this experience of a larger reality is what results in brain changes. This is different than thinking that brain changes brought on by meditation cause a delusional thinking, of seeing ourselves connected to the world. Rather the mind-body meditative experience gives us a chance to see through the veils and experience a deeper reality. This repeated experience is what physically changes the brain, just as the physical reality of pianists' repeated thumb/finger strikes change their neural wiring.

For me, after having my experience, the field is real. I would be lying to you and to myself if I said I have any doubt of its reality. For Lao Tzu and Taoist philosophers it was/is real. Lao Tzu told us that the stirrings, the inspiration of the heart, could be heard by the whole universe. This reality is at the heart of Taoist and Tai Chi imagery in the Yin Yang symbol. Again, the smaller Yin Yang symbols in the dots of the white and black wave, are meant to show how the microcosms of experience ripple throughout the macrocosm of society, the world, and the universe. Our heart, mind and universe are connected according to Taoist philosophy.

Lao Tzu said that the Tao operates always, everywhere, throughout the universe. But it is formless, nebulous, and without sound – a quantum field perhaps, as the quantum field appears to be nothing. Yet all particles that form the manifest world we see emerge from this field, just as Lao Tzu claimed the Tao, the energetic way of the universe, is the mother of all things. The Tao, the field, connects us all to everything. When we let go and allow our Tai Chi to flow us, we merge with the field. We attune to the flow, the currents of the universe, and in those moments are more close to reality than at any other moments in our lives.

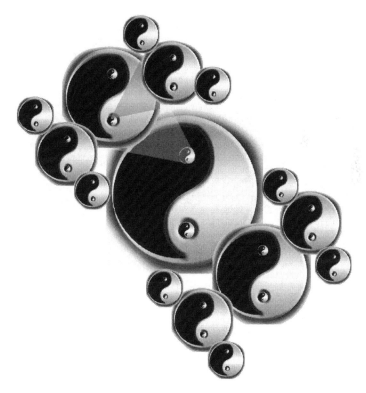

I think it was critical that this ethereal experience opened my upper and middle Dan Tiens, the mind and the heart Dan Tien. Most of Tai Chi teaching focuses almost exclusively on the lower Dan Tien, where our movements come from, the physical Dan Tien.

My Tai Chi teacher had told me before my own awakening that Tai Chi's greatest power is to bring "higher states of awareness" into our physical lives.

This opening of my upper and middle Dan Tiens changed everything for me in many ways that would unfold for many years later. When I first pitched the idea of a World Tai Chi & Qigong Day to the annual national conference of the National Qigong Association, a page would turn. Master Li Junfeng would speak before I did. Master Li's story was one of opening to the middle Dan Tien, the heart, the energy of love.

Master Li had been one of China's greatest Wushu coaches, until he had an epiphany, and he left his martial arts career to dedicate his life to expanding love in the world via his Qigong teaching.

After I made my pitch for other Tai Chi and Qigong teachers to join in on this World Tai Chi & Qigong Day idea I had, Master Li approached me in the hall as we all exited the room where the plenary session speeches were given. He extolled me, "This world event you want to create. If you do it, do it for love, or don't do it at all."

His words vibrated through me and affected everything for all of these years of global organizing. After that meeting, our motto would become "One World … One Breath." I believe these events were all connected, my angel's breathing lesson as a boy, the angel's opening my heart Dan Tien, and Master Li pleading with me to make love central to my global organizing efforts. Dr. Effie Chow, founder of the World Congress on Qigong would also later implore me to make love central.

As my Tai Chi teacher imparted to me again and again, Tai Chi's gift is to make the higher dimensions of awareness tangible and manifest – making higher states of consciousness grounded. As Tai Chi players, opening in our Nei Gong or Sitting Qigong meditations to our upper and middle Dan Tien energy, our higher mind and heart energy, can then weave through our lower Dan Tien's flowing Tai Chi movements to bring a higher possibility into this life, into our arts.

World Tai Chi & Qigong Day 2016 event joins
100s of cities, and over 80 nations' events

"One World ... One Breath"

[photos courtesy of Ahmed Shaaban and Ahmed El Rouby]

A Taoist Way of Life ...

It was at this time, after this ethereal experience, that I came the closest to living as a Taoist monk would. It changed everything. My Tai Chi journey would be forever affected in profound ways by this Taoist time.

After my "expansion" experience and writing the poem in the previous chapter about the revelation the angel seemed to be here to provide, of awakening us up to our connection to all of life, I wrote non-stop for months after that. Writing thoughts and feelings down in the car on the way to work, at work, on breaks, at home, and waking up in the night with ideas I would write down.

The following weeks were also a period of tremendous grace. Allowing my most authentic feelings to come through me. To surface and to be expressed through my hand on paper, which enabled a greater flow to come through me.

I was unhinged from the rat race. I turned off my TV and radio, and cancelled my newspaper subscription and turned away from the things of man. When I wasn't writing, I was walking, jogging, meditating, or sitting on the beach watching the ocean waves.

I turned away from the things of man, and turned inward for months. Huge shifts in my perception and my reality occurred at this time. It was an organic Taoist way of life, spending all my time sensing the "flow" of the universe. Not pushing, rushing, or forming thoughts, but rather opening to the internal rhythms flowing through me. Feeling emotions, feeling sensations, not controlling, not directing, just *being*. I have never done this again for such a prolonged period of time in my life. But my life, my Tai Chi, my teaching and writing is still profoundly impacted by the insights these months gave me. Not intellectually so much as viscerally, feeling what it feels like to let go of control, and to flow – which is what Tai Chi training is about at its deepest core.

When there are no distractions life comes at you powerfully, deeply, and often hard fisted. You begin to become conscious of transgressions you made against others in your life. Often not spitefully or with malice, but just unconsciously. When there are no distractions you become conscious. Enlightenment can be painful and filled with upheaval. You have to feel the waves come through your mind and heart, and you often cringe in shame of what you learn of yourself, of your past unconsciousness. Then, ultimately, you have to forgive yourself and move on, changed by your awakening forever. You start to realize that it is okay to see mistakes and to regret, and to change, and to forgive, and to move on. This de-rigidifies your world and allows a renewed sense of flow in your mind, heart, and body, that can greatly enhance the liquidity and power of your Tai Chi. Allowing the energy to flow through without resisting it or the changes it brings. And when we come out on the other side of enlightenment, even though the process can at times be painful. A sense of grace follows in its wake. A larger lighter sense of being emerges, a greater sense of flow and surrender.

During this time when I turned from the things of man, and went within, I was so kind and patient. I remember that when I was writing and my children would interrupt me, I would stop what I was doing, and "be with them" in a way I never had before. My normal irritation when interrupted was no longer there. I was open, in no hurry, in flow, in grace. This new consciousness really loosened up my Tai Chi forms over the years, showing me that a loose mind, a loose heart, translates into a looser body, and more liquid and flowing and powerful Tai Chi.

Back when all this was happening, I would talk, really talk, and really be with people at work. This became a training in Ch'an, or Zen, the art of "being in the moment."

My coworkers and even strangers would open up to me and tell me deep spiritual things that nobody talked about with co-workers, let alone strangers. A janitor confided to me at work in the hallway that he had cancer, and that he'd prayed for strength to quit smoking and his urge went away. A man at a doctor's office I went to, in order to take the company mandatory periodic drug test, told me he had just gotten out of prison and felt bad, because he was imposing on his friend and the friend's wife who were putting him up to help him get started. I told him not to worry, he was getting on the right track. And it was okay for his friends to help him because the only reason we are here on this planet is to help one another, and he should not feel bad about letting his friends help him. I could see the relief on his young troubled face. Coworkers would drift into my office and tell me about challenges they faced in their marriages, or as parents or in their spiritual lives, and I would open up to them and share the grace and compassion I was feeling. And I could see the relief in their eyes and on their faces, seeing their shoulders relax down away from their neck – just as we as teachers often see our Tai Chi student's shoulders relax down away from their neck as we instruct them in breathing, and letting go, and sinking into our postures.

During this period of grace, every old person I saw looked like my parents, and every child I saw looked like my lost son Isaac. My heart was as big as the world. I was fragile and open. I stayed clear like this for months, until I eventually began to slip back into the world, into the ways of man. I could feel my mind, heart and body tightening. But I never saw the world exactly the same way as I had before all this happened. My mind was always more open, my heart more open and fragile, my body and my Tai Chi forms more loose and flowing. Once a mind is lighted, it can never be squeezed back into its old reality. Not completely anyway.

NOW HERE'S WHAT IS REALLY AMAZING. During this time of grace when I was obsessed with writing down all the thoughts, feelings and images coming into my mind, all this writing began to pile up during these months of obsessive writing. And it became a book on children's innocent wisdom and what it offers the world, and poems and stories about people's feelings. I had never been a writer prior to this event, and no one outside my wife and kids knew what had happened to me, or that I was now obsessively writing. I wasn't telling anyone because it all felt so strange and weird to me at the time.

Finally, one night after months of writing, I began to doubt myself completely. *Why was I doing this? It didn't make me any money or make any logical (Yang) sense in my life.* All this Yin opening to feelings and perceptions had no logical relevance to me, my family, or my practical life. I was about to give up. Then, the phone rang. It was my sister in Kansas, and it was the strangest phone call I ever had. It wasn't strange just because in all the years I had been in California this sister had never called me. It was far more bizarre than that.

My sister seemed rushed to get something out; she said that our mother who had died months before had come to her in a dream last night. She said Mom had taken her into a pure white room, and in the center of the room was a stack of white papers with writing on them. And she said Mom had begun to flip through the papers telling my sister, "Look, look what Junior's been doing."

At this point, I was woozy. My forehead was perspiring, as my sister told me that our mother who had passed away had been watching what I was doing, and seemed to be excited and proud of it. I had to press on and find out if this was real. It felt like it couldn't be real.

I asked my sister, "What was on the papers?"

She said, "Oh, there were so many, I'm not sure ... wait! I remember there were lots of poems, poems and stories about peoples' feelings, and stories about children's innocent wisdom and what it offers the world."

My knees nearly buckled. I had to hold onto my bed's headboard to keep from falling. *It was real, this was real!* There is no way my sister could have A) known I was writing, and B) that I had recently written a big stack of things, and C) known I had been writing poems and stories about people's feelings, and about how children's innocent wisdom is needed in the world.

That writing eventually became a book. But this *event* that got me started as a writer that night became the catalyst that led to me writing about Tai Chi and Qigong, and to writing a globally published book in several languages on the Internal Arts. And in time, writing a website that would connect the global Tai Chi and Qigong family.

I know that this "expansion of mind and heart event" prepared me to eventually create a world event of personal and global health and healing. Because that event made my mind deaf to national borders and racial and religious and ethnic divisions. It prepared me for the many years of forming World Tai Chi & Qigong Day, where I would travel the world, and meet online, and sometimes in person, with people all over the planet. And connect with them in ways that often lasted for many years, and changed the way we all saw the world.

And I think that expansion experience is what would give this event the motto of "One World ... One Breath" in recognition of Qigong meaning "breath work" or "life energy work." And in recognition of the angel's breathing lesson, and of this lesson of how when we breathe and let go, we merge in some way with "the field" that connects all of us, everything, everywhere.

As a 6 year old boy, that angel had taught me that "the breath" is what can connect the logical, linear material world we live in, with the ethereal, energetic, spiritual aspect of our being and world. The goal of World Tai Chi & Qigong Day evolved into working towards getting institutions and governments to expand mind-body meditative practices (which all focus on the breath) into society at all levels. And in our small way has made huge inroads into making this happen.

As you read before, 22 US governors officially proclaimed, not only World Tai Chi & Qigong Day as a celebration, but recognized the value of Tai Chi and Qigong for their citizens. Also, many senates, including California, Puerto Rico, and New York have done so. As well as the National Congress of Brazil (National Council of Deputies). Government institutions, ministries, consulates and embassies of many nations have supported this movement.

Now I have to remind you that Tai Chi and Qigong ARE NOT RELIGIONS, AND ARE NOT RELIGIOUS PRACTICES. They are mind-body neurological science, which can be done in a purely secular science based way, and can be taught thus in public schools. Tai Chi and Qigong are practiced worldwide by Atheists, Agnostics, Jews, Christians, Muslims, Buddhists, etc. Often all those people may be in the very same classroom doing it together.

The science is in on Tai Chi and Qigong, as well as mind-body meditative benefits for the brain, the nervous system, the immune system and general health. And also for emotional and mental health. They make the brain bigger and make it work better. No religious dogma is invoked at any time in these practices. They are in fact the opposite of dogma.

Having said that, Tai Chi is today being taught in Mosques, Temples, Churches, and the like. They can be a great compliment to one's spiritual journey. But all Tai Chi and Qigong do is cleanse the system of stress, so that we can be the most real we can be, whether that is in pursuing secular tasks, secular education, or for those so inclined, to add to their spiritual life.

My point is, that given the scientific research we now have on Tai Chi, Qigong, and mind-body meditation techniques, it is literally quite insane that they are not already part of public education. They are proven to help reduce ADHD symptoms in youth, improve the ability to process and retain information, expand creativity, and reduce violent tendencies, which would profoundly help with bullying issues in school. It already is having such effects in the schools that are now using these mind-body science based tools.

In the end, it would create a generation much less plagued by social ills. The Dalai Lama said that if we taught all school children meditation, that violence would become a thing of the past. Doing so would also save global society trillions of dollars in saved health costs year after year after year.

I want to note something, because I do not want this book and my story of "spiritual" experiences to interfere with the work and the world of World Tai Chi & Qigong Day. I am only sharing my *personal* spiritual story here, for those who would benefit from it. This has no bearing on our work as a World Tai Chi & Qigong Day collective, because our work is secular, and we provide medical research data to Tai Chi and Qigong enthusiasts, professionals, and to institutions and government worldwide. Our collective efforts are purely secular in nature, and science based.

However, my life has involved observing the evolution of science, quantum physics, chaos mathematics, neural science research, and the like, looking for answers. And finding that ancient concepts we once thought of as "mystical" (like the benefits of meditative practices and the Tao's energetic nature of the universe and the Yin Yang forces of nature and the Yin Yang symbol's self-replicating quality), are being validated by the evolution of science. As science becomes subtle enough to see what was seen thousands of years ago by those going within, to study the physical universe from the most immediate venue – within the human mind and body.

So perhaps one day we may find that these experiences I had as a 6 year old, and in my mid-20s, that changed the course of my life and affected the world, may one day become understandable by science. My life has taught me that science is not the totality of reality. Science is what we are able to quantify and understand about reality at this moment. Things we experience beyond what falls within those definable parameters are often called "mystical," and by many of those who have not had those experiences, are simply dismissed.

In my 40 years I have seen science's ability to measure, quantify, and understand expanding, as science and technology are expanding their awareness and ability faster than at any time in human history. The speed of technological change is doubling every 18 months today – and this is as slow as it will ever get.

In these 40 years I have seen Tai Chi and Qigong's ancient concepts validated again and again. Less and less people laugh at it, because modern technological science has caught up with these ancient internal mind-body sciences. Tai Chi and Qigong have not changed – modern science has changed and evolved, and it will continue to do so.

For example, the concept of Qi, or life energy, was dismissed by most people when I began learning Tai Chi Meditation 40 years ago. Yet today, aspects of it are scientifically detectable and measurable, finding that human energy emissions Tai Chi players call Qi contain infra-red and increased biophoton emissions.

The other night I was doing Tai Chi in the local park just as the sun was going down. As I flowed through the forms, as my arms and hands flowed with the dark green forest of trees behind them, I would glimpse subtle radiance. Not that I could stare at, but that would pass through my peripheral vision like an airy mist at moments. When I first saw it many years ago, it felt like a miracle. Yet perhaps I am glimpsing the "photons," the "light particles" human emitted energy can contain. Perhaps Tai Chi affects the body in ways that affect the eyes, and how they perceive subtleties like these photons. Or maybe when doing Tai Chi more photons are emitted, as research shows Qigong can do.

When you do Tai Chi for decades, eventually you get a sense of the movements moving you, flowing you in rhythms and patterns. Like your body is being drawn on tracks that have been laid, flowing on airy ribbons and a sense of power and energy, which flows through you as you are carried by these sensations.

I am convinced that one day a computer device will be able to detect these currents and flows of energy that pass through and expand from a Tai Chi player, and one day anyone will be able to see this light show on a computer monitor's screen.

I have found over the decades of Tai Chi Meditation teaching, that my period of tremendous grace, following my enlightening experience that led to a Taoist way of life for months, has powerfully impacted my Tai Chi teaching. That period of months so long ago, when I was allowing my most authentic feelings to come through me, to surface, and to be expressed through my hand on paper, enabled a greater flow to come through me.

This physically affected my Tai Chi. I became less censored and more authentic, allowing the true me to flow through me mentally, emotionally and physically. It was like opening a gate to the flow of Qi and the Tao, the energetic flow of the universe.

When I heard a rapper say that he was "spitting his flow," it made perfect sense to me. I knew that feeling of relaxing out of the way of what I was here to witness as a human being on this planet, so it could flow through me, and I could "testify." I found Tai Chi to be a model for relaxing out of the way, to feel the flow flowing through us, or trying to flow through us, waiting for us to let go and relax out of the way.

My actions and words became more powerful, and my approach to teaching Tai Chi and Meditation became vastly more expansive, uncensored by what I thought people might think. I followed my internal rhythms and senses of what Tai Chi and Meditation meant to me, and how it felt to me when I was doing it – trying to reveal all and be authentic with students. And they resonated with it. My classes got bigger and bigger, and people got more and deeper benefits from the classes, literally changing people's lives.

Today, when I walk into a class I have zero agenda, no game plan of what will happen in that class. I breathe and let go and open to a flow that occurs, formed by the Tao, by the people in the class, and by my un-gripped flowing self. We ride nebulous waves rather than follow lines painted on the proverbial floor.

It is scary to do this. It requires faith, and it requires us to be centered as teachers, yet vulnerable and willing to look the fool should it happen. In the end, this actually lightens the class. I have found people resonate to authenticity and vulnerability. The energy in the room feels so much different today than when I first began teaching, when my teaching was Yang and left brain and mental, rather than Yin and flowing and nebulous.

My classes are so much more fun when we flow in the Tao, and I let go of control. This is the way of the Tao, this is the way of Tai Chi.

The Tao of Science

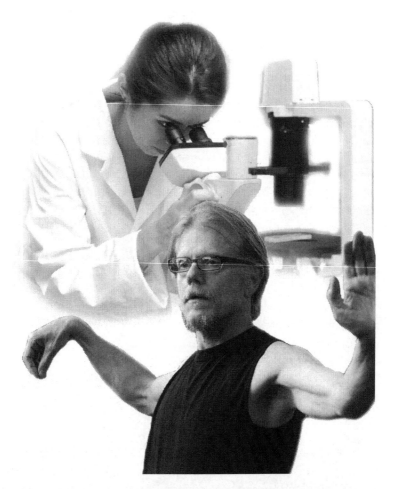

Once again, I want to be *perfectly* clear – I share these personal experiences I had in this book, that have been part of my personal journey, for my own clarification, and as a validation to those of you who may resonate with this on a personal level. Or perhaps expand your perception of the world in some way, if it is new to you.

I do not, however, share all of this in my classes, although they do color the way I teach. I am constantly imploring students to move into "what they feel" and beyond "what they think," so they can have an untethered Yin non-analytical experience. In that way I think these experiences I don't talk about have helped me to be a better teacher.

But again, for clarity, I don't normally share my angelic experiences in my classes. My classes, like World Tai Chi & Qigong Day's global health education efforts, are secular and science-based. I inform my students of "the science" of Tai Chi, Qigong, and mind body meditative practices. I teach in public schools and in some of the world's largest health institutions.

Having said that, my experiences, which I believe Tai Chi and Qigong did not "cause," but may have loosened me up in order to experience, have given me a deeper understanding of Taoist philosophy and how Tai Chi can complement that. It has also helped me to see how Taoist philosophy can complement one's Tai Chi journey. Again, I do not see Taoism as a religion. I think it is wholly inaccurate to characterize it as such. I see Taoism as a high science, one that modern science is only beginning to wrap its head around.

As I mentioned earlier, when I learned that ancient Acupuncture Points are located often on "points of least electrical resistance" on the skin, it made me wonder just what was at work with those early Chinese researchers millennia before. When you look at how Taoist's Yin Yang symbol represented how everything in the universe is made up of positive and negative polarities, and now modern physics shows us that every single thing in the universe is made up of the positive and negative polarities of subatomic particles, it makes you wonder, doesn't it? How did they sense this?

Is it possible that, as Taoist philosophy extolls, that by looking within we see the entire world? In the East ancient mystics were touching into profound physics and mathematical insights, that millennia later modern physicists and mathematicians using computer equipment would validate. One looking from the inside out at the "star stuff within us," as renowned astrophysicist Carl Sagan reminded us that we are made of. The other looking from the outside in with modern technological equipment. It is widely accepted that the most sophisticated computer in the world is the human brain. A system we are only just beginning to understand. And the more we do, the more we understand how ancient wisdom on mind body technologies is profound.

Look within to see universe

My personal ethereal experiences as a child and a young adult showed me, or enabled me to "feel," what Einstein was talking about when he said that "we are connected" to others and to nature, and it is a delusion to think we are separate. But, just as I am sure Einstein did not regularly expound on his personal realization when giving physics lectures at the university, I do not expound on my own spiritual insights in my university or other Tai Chi classes.

Yet being deeply drawn to quantum physics and modern chaos mathematics *because* my own personal ethereal experiences, I believe, have given me insight into how Taoism and related philosophies are high science. I am drawn to using science to try to understand on a left-brain Yang level, the depth and breadth of the Yin right-brain experiences, which science isn't able to understand (as yet), but can measure the physical benefits it offers those who practice these arts.

My ethereal experience where I felt connected to everything when I lost my sense of self, and merged with a field of existence, drew me to exploring the Quantum Field and how it connects everything. In physics researchers have found that subatomic particles can have a non-local effect on other particles at great distances. This effect occurs instantaneously, faster than the speed of light. This means just what Einstein said, 'we are connected to everything.' Physical objects like human beings and the human mind are connected by an unseen field, and science is only in the beginnings of unraveling what this means.

The Global Consciousness Project, which sprung from research at Princeton University on 'whether human consciousness affects electronic equipment like computers,' later expanded to discover that when human consciousness is focused en masse, it affects computers known as Random Event Generators all over the world.

I personally wonder if the consciousness events I and my wife had as children (see earlier chapters) were coincidence, or if those events were connected, designed in some way to "connect us" 15 years later, when we would both end up at the same university. Thousands of miles away from my wife's garden where she had her ethereal experience as a child in 1963, the same time when I had mine. I wonder if the ethereal experience I had in my 20s, of feeling connected to people all over the planet, somehow laid the tracks for me to meet people all over the world. And if that had an impact on our idea of a global health and healing event, electrifying those people who learned about it worldwide when we began announcing it.

Taoist philosophy is about the connection of all things via a field, an unseen, intangible, nebulous field that permeates all existence.

I briefly alluded to what Einstein called the "spooky effect," in reference to nonlocality research in physics. Researchers found that when particles were affected or stimulated in some way, that they could find particles great distances away that would react at precisely the same instant.

What made this significant is that the reaction happened "faster than the speed of light." As far as known physics knows, nothing can move faster than the speed of light. So this means that no actual connection between these particles, no type of communication, could have been possible. In other words, it appears to mean that the very fabric of the universe is all connected, which is what Taoism has understood for thousands of years, long before particle physics came into being.

I realized human consciousness may be part of this, becoming aware of research done at Princeton University, which eventually evolved into what was called The Global Consciousness Project. The GCP discovering when humanity focused their minds en masse, it affected computers all across the planet simultaneously. The original research was to determine if electronics were affected by human consciousness. I think many of us have wondered that, at times when our computer malfunctions when we are the most stressed out—in other words, at the worst possible moment. Then we laugh at ourselves for thinking such a wild thing, that our minds could affect our computers. Turns out we may not have been so crazy to think that after all.

However, the Global Consciousness Project's work expanded beyond that issue, when they placed electronic devices known as Random Event Generators (REGs) all over the planet. Researchers found, as I mentioned above, that when humanity focused their minds en masse, it caused all of their REGs to go off course. Princess Diana's death, and the World Trade Center collapses, were among the events the project found set off their electronic devices.

This would lead to the conclusion that when Taoists spoke or wrote about all beings being connected in a real way, it was not just flowery poetry, but perhaps actual physics they were able to tune into with their consciousness. As you read before, Einstein believed that our feeling of separation was a delusion that we should overcome.

Biologist Rupert Sheldrake wrote about some interesting events involving rat studies using mazes, to observe how fast rats could learn. He wrote that it was interesting that when rats in a Harvard laboratory suddenly began to learn a maze pattern more quickly, rats in other university studies in Scotland and Australia suddenly also learned the maze more quickly as well.

One personal anecdotal synchronous event I experienced made me wonder about the concept of group mind as well. I am not referring to the event in 1963, when both I and my wife had spiritual visions that same year as children on opposite sides of the planet (mentioned earlier in the book). Although this is an amazing coincidence in itself. Rather, I was intrigued when I traveled to Hong Kong in 2013 and toured the Hong Kong Polytechnic University's Tai Chi Research Laboratory. I learned from one of the researchers there that a landmark event had occurred in 1998, when a new director took over research at the university and began raising funds to research Tai Chi as part of Chinese Medicine research. This event had global ramifications, as the Hong Kong researchers published papers on Tai Chi's effect on mental acuity – research that would be read by researchers worldwide in universities around the planet.

It struck me to learn when Hong Kong Polytechnic's historic research began, because the year *1998* was also the very first mass Tai Chi and Qigong event, which spawned World Tai Chi & Qigong Day in 80 nations over the coming years. Then the hair raised a bit on my arm, when I also discovered that the very first official World Congress on Qigong, organized by Dr. Effie Chow's organization, was held in *1998*. This was an even vaster deal than the establishment of the World Congress, because this would quickly lead to Dr. Effie Chow being appointed by President Clinton, to the original 15 member White House Commission on Complementary and Alternative Medicine Policy.

None of us even knew each other at the time all this was happening, all in the same year. It seems like such a *vast* coincidence that: 1) in 1998 a major technical research university would launch a pioneering research project designed to unite Eastern and Western medical approaches involving Tai Chi, which would influence researchers worldwide. And 2) a World Congress on Qigong was founded, an event designed specifically to connect scientists studying Tai Chi and Qigong with Tai Chi and Qigong masters and professionals from around the world. An event that would have huge global implications over the years in and of itself, let alone with it resulting in Dr. Chow being appointed to what would be the very first in history President's Commission on Complementary and Alternative Medicine Policy.

And then on top of that, in 1998 World Tai Chi & Qigong Day was born, an event designed to connect Tai Chi and Qigong enthusiasts, teachers, and organizations worldwide, and to train them in collecting this newly emerging scientific research, and in creating mass media events all over the planet to educate millions of the hard science being done by research universities. And also to training the world family of Tai Chi and Qigong in how to use that emerging science to create an avalanche of official bodies worldwide advocating Tai Chi and Qigong for their citizens. Leading to 22 US governors; the senates and/or legislatures of many states and beyond, including California, New York, and Puerto Rico; the National Congress of Brazil; and government ministries and agencies and consulates from India to China to Egypt, Europe, Asia, Australia, Africa and Latin America — all officially advocating the benefits of Tai Chi and Qigong to their citizens.

What are the odds that all of these mutually supportive world influencing events would come into being in the same year? Realize, Tai Chi and Qigong had been around for hundreds and thousands of years, respectively. This mass global expanse of their influence had never happened at this accelerated rate in all of those years. Then in one year three events that would very literally become world altering occurred. A more elegant plan could have never been designed — yet it happened as if a master planner had thought it all out to all happen at just the right moment in human history. In coming years this rapid expanse of Internal Arts, according to medical research, could end up saving global society literally *trillions* of dollars in saved health costs.

Given the scientific research of the Global Consciousness Project, and the rat studies mentioned above, it makes you wonder if synchronous events like this that literally change human history, might be an indication that the waves of consciousness do not stay contained inside the human skull. Just as Lao Tzu described our connection to everything and how we could affect the world by going within.

Consider this; if the (albeit very intellectual) Harvard rats getting smarter about a maze they were trying to break through could affect rats in universities in Scotland and Australia, couldn't it be that human beings, around the planet poised in key places at a key moment in human history, seeing a new way for society and humanity that will one day lead to trillions of dollars in health cost savings worldwide each year — might likewise have shared that new knowledge with one another? The way the smart Harvard rats did? I do believe that if Lao Tzu was around today, he would answer that question the way Master Po had answered Grasshopper's question (of 'how is it possible you can feel your heartbeat master?') with a question of his own.

Lao Tzu would ask us why we think it so difficult to entertain a reality that consciousness radiates outward. Or more precisely, given physics' nonlocality data, that consciousness is simply *all connected all the time*—just as Lao Tzu had tried to tell us. Just as matter in the universe appears to be connected, according to physics' discovery of the universal connection of matter shown in nonlocality research, which Einstein dubbed the "spooky effect."

The amazing unfolding of the Yin Yang and Tai Chi symbol at the heart of Taoist thought does not stop with consciousness and physics research. Taoist concepts also appear to have a real and deep connection with modern Chaos Mathematics' "self-replicating theory."

Chaosticians have noted that reality is self-replicating. Gross examples of this are seen in how the veins of an oak tree's leaf resemble the structure of the tree, with a main stem, and branching out in to smaller veins, just like the trees branches do. The leaf's image would represent a microcosmic view, while the tree would be the macrocosm. Another example is found if you look at a microscopic view of a grain of sand, or a rock on a beach. And then look at the macrocosmic view of an aerial photo of the beach line, and note how similar they are.

Chaos Mathematicians create computer models of living systems using ever changing mathematical formulas, and then make them visual by compressing the data to create images known as "fractal images," otherwise known as fractal art. You have seen them, they are all over popular culture. If you can't place fractal art in your mind off the top of your head, realize that they often look a lot like the old paisley print shirts many of us wore back in the day, back in times of wilder fashion.

Chaos Mathematics' Self Replicating Theory, Taoism, Qi, Qigong

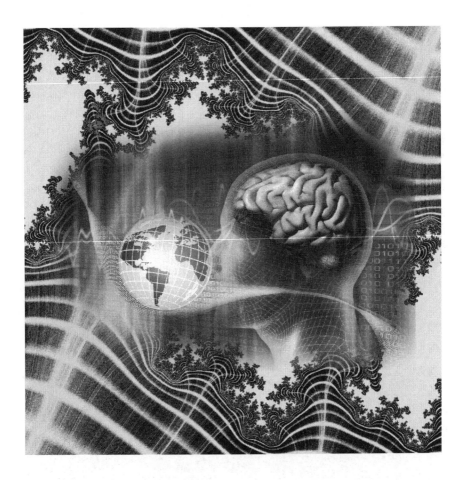

One way that these angelic experiences I had have profoundly affected and improved my teaching, is by allowing me to actually feel the "field," the Tao, the energetic nature of reality, and how all things, all of us, are connected. When my Upper Dan Tien and Middle Dan Tien's mind and heart energy expanded, and I became that expansion, and was able to "feel the hearts of people worldwide," I had a tangible experience of what modern Chaos Mathematicians and the ancient Taoist's were referring to in their "self-replicating nature of the universe" concepts or theory.

Since having that experience, my own meditations changed profoundly. The way I teach Qigong and Nei Gong have as well. When I first started learning Sitting Qigong and Nei Gong in my Tai Chi Meditation training, I thought in Yang, analytical ways. I imagined the Upper and Middle and Lower Dan Tiens as maybe three inch finite locations in space within my body. My mind thereby limited what they were, and in fact got in the way of my being able to actually experience the Dan Tien's true nature. I was "holding or controlling" the experience, making mental pictures in my mind that I held in concentration, in order to have the meditative experience of the Dan Tiens.

However, after my "expansion" experience with the Upper and Middle Dan Tiens, I realized that these energy centers are "all encompassing." When I think of my Upper Dan Tien now, my mind does think of that location in the center of the brain, but then quickly "freefalls" into the experience of light or energy within that energy center, and the experience is all encompassing. I feel the sensation of the light or energy everywhere throughout my physical body, but beyond, limitless, undefinable – a freefall experience of absolute letting go. I now use that term in my classes. During Nei Gong meditation I frequently use the term "free fall," a connotation of an "absolute letting go."

When I sat in my bedroom in California that night, yet expanded beyond the planet, becoming vast and open and undefined, I had a veil removed, and saw what the energy centers we call the Dan Tiens are. Not just three-dimensional orbs inside our body, but "portals," to our macrocosmic connection with everything. Yes, they are deep within us, but they also are the farthest reaches of reality, out there. This is what Taoist philosophy tells us, that within us is the universe. Our Dan Tiens are not finite places in space, limited to a 2 or 3 inch sphere of energy, they are portals, and when we experience them and then absolutely "let go" we can freefall into amazing experiences.

One thing I forgot to mention in my remembrance of my angelic Upper/Middle Dan Tien experience, was what the "being" told me, just before it touched me in the center of my brain or Upper Dan Tien. It told me, "I am about to show you what life *could* be like." And then my Upper Dan Tien exploded in that soft ethereal super nova. That was the *first* thing it told me before giving me that experience. The *last* thing it told me after I had become afraid, tightened up and held my breath (resulting in everything, my expansion, collapsing and me slamming back down into my body), the last message it gave me was, "Fear closes all doors. Fear closes all doors."

Experiencing the Dan Tiens and other energy centers like portals requires a surrender, and absolute letting go. I had yet another experience with this being when I was near Aspen, Colorado, at a personal expansion symposium high up in the Rocky Mountains. At night I slept in a loft bedroom with a wall of windows overlooking the Crystal River. The river babbled loudly with the sounds of melting mountain runoff down to the plains below. The sound was a beautiful way to sleep as the frozen water became fluid, swirling over, around, and between the rocks below my window.

At about 3 a.m. (these events seemed to come at 3 a.m., perhaps when my mind and body let go the most), I felt something happening. Something, an energy, building and amassing above my head as I lay in my bed in the loft above the river, with a platinum moon shining down through the windows. There was a throbbing intensity to it.

The intensity gave me pause. I had a sense that if I "opened my mind" and accepted this experience, that something big and huge would occur. But I had to *allow* it to happen. I lay there in the dark with this vast thing about to occur, and I agreed to let it occur, *tentatively*.

The top of my head opened and it was like a jet engine revved up, and something, some energetic download, poured into my head, my mind. But it stopped almost immediately. I had been trying to let this event happen, but at the same time keep control, keep my left-brain analytical control and analysis going, so that I could be in control and decide how I wanted this to go.

The being informed me that the energy cannot work this way. It requires faith, absolute faith, and you cannot hedge your bets. It wasn't a test; it was just the way the energy worked. As I lay there so many things passed through my mind in a matter of seconds. I remembered all the "tests of faith" I had read about in my religious education in Sunday school, Bible school, and Confirmation. And then I remembered an Einstein quote that had stuck in my mind: "The most important question you can ask yourself is 'Is the universe a friendly place?'" Einstein said this is most important, because all our life will unfold from how we answer that question.

What was about to happen, if I chose to let it happen, was like a doorway or portal that could only be opened by the state of my mind, my consciousness, and I had to be "all in, or all out." What I would realize later is that the experience I was about to be given was so much vaster than my current state of thinking. That the hallways, walls, and structure of my mind would have to completely melt away in order for the "new reality" to have space to expand through me, and in a way, become me, thoroughly transforming me on a universal level.

I began to think that perhaps those "tests of faith" I had read about in my religious education weren't the acts of a petty God, demanding absolute obedience from his subjects or pets. No, I began to see that "absolute faith" was a prerequisite for the mind being able to open to larger realities.

One neurological study, that would catch my eye years later, was about how regular meditation changes the brain structure. <u>Part of the brain reflexively rejects new information, new paradigms of reality. Meditation practice changed the neurology of the test subjects' brain.</u> This study and the effects they were studying are called <u>neuroplasticity.</u> Meditation caused that "auto-rejection of new paradigms, new information" to go into abeyance, allowing meditator's brains to "ponder new information" before rejecting it, and this practice physically re-wires the brain. {meditation}

I began to see these "spiritual" events with an "eye of science" over my 40 years of research into my own consciousness, and also through my professional life, following cutting edge neurological and health science research. I began to see "faith" as less of a petty God's demand of absolute obedience from God's subjects, controlled like bovine sub-creatures, and more like a benevolent mentor who was trying to help us see a larger world.

You see, "faith" as this "being" that has mentored me for nearly 55 years of my life over the course of these extraordinary events, made it clear that night that I could not "hold on to control," if I was going to experience this reality so much larger than I currently held. It wasn't that I was being tested; it wasn't that obedience was being demanded of me. It was because as any mathematician knows, "a set cannot contain itself." Our conscious, our analytical, left-brain, Yang, control thinking, is our "set of reality." If a larger paradigm, or larger Reality Set is to be allowed to fill us, to fill our consciousness and our being, we have to completely "let go" of the old set, the previous paradigm. Let go of the old reality, in order to become pliant and fluid enough to become larger. This information was not about a "new thought" to be held in the head like a shiny bobble on the mind's existing shelves. It was about allowing the rigid shack of my mind to be blown apart to make space for a multi-dimensional palace of crystalline possibility to shine in blazing colors that could not be held by my mind's old walls. This wasn't a "new trick" I was being given, it was an opportunity for profound personal transformation, and evolution into a completely new state of being.

When I did let go, and allowed this thing to happen – absolutely letting go and having faith and trusting in the benevolence of the universe – well, words can never come close to conveying what I felt.

Once I had surrendered, it was as if that jet engine that had revved up for a moment, before I tried to "keep control," had now been thrown into full throttle. My mind was now in the center of a blasting jet engine. I felt like some kind of cosmic computer download was pouring into me, not just my physical body but my expansive energy being. It was cataclysmic, epic, on the edge of tearing everything I was apart. I felt as if every DNA cell in my body were being transformed in some profound and fundamental way, and much more than that. The energetic field from where my atoms emerge, that form my molecules that form my cells, was being completely electrified and that a metamorphosis far beyond what my puny words could ever convey was occurring.

I could not imagine how this could go on without tearing the house apart. It was so vast, violent and earth shattering in magnitude. I have never felt anything that came close to it, even on two occasions when I have been caught in tornados. In one case I felt the tornado come over the freeway underpass I was wedged under. Again, words fail me – huge, vast, terrible, beautiful, destruction, birth, evolution, transformation – are feeble attempts.

Then, it was over. I lay there in my bed gasping. The house was silent. No one was up but me. It had woken no one. I lay there for hours listening to the Crystal River and the Rocky Mountains babble their knowing song to me, buzzing in – a *newness*.

I do not tell this story in my classes. However, my meditation changed profoundly after this. When I invoked that Upper or Middle Dan Tien or other energy centers, it was only left-brain Yang thought at that initial moment. Then my goal was to sigh, to surrender into a "freefall" into the light, the energy, the expanding radiance – all encompassing, my whole being surrendering to it. I no longer "held" an idea of a three inch orb of energy when doing Nei Gong meditation involving the Dan Tiens or energy centers. Again, it became all-encompassing and a freefall. Don't get me wrong – I don't normally have experiences of the intensity I had with this being at 3 a.m. on those few nights in my life. Like everyone, I drift in and out of meditative states. Sometimes catching myself ponder if I forgot to feed the dog or some such worry, as I meditate.

So I don't "live" in this other world of vastness. My meditations struggle with drifting in and out of worry and distraction, just like anyone else's meditations do. So I'm very understanding and compassionate of my student's struggles with meditation, and I share with them my own challenges of drifting consciousness and distractions.

But, like I said, these experiences colored my view of what the Dan Tiens are, and what meditation and Nei Gong energy work are. It left me with a larger vernacular, like "freefall" and "surrender," that has really helped me connect with many more people than I would have before having these experiences. My students often have profound experiences of their own. I don't make it happen, they let it happen. It is *their* experience.

This experience with the energy download that began with me trying to "hedge" the experience by having it, but not totally surrendering into it, has profoundly changed my approach to teaching. The three words my students here again and again, is "just let go." That experience which required my absolute surrender into the experience if I was to have it, opened me to how to get the most out of mind-body experiences like

Qigong or Tai Chi. Letting go, and surrendering into the experience totally is what I and my students strive for.

If my religious students discuss trepidations to letting go, I simply invite them to invoke the trust in their benevolent faith to initiate their experience, so they can have faith and trust in absolutely letting go. Like I said, it is *their* experience, not mine. But, fear will stop it, so whatever can help a student let go of their fear and freefall, facilitates their brain falling into the alpha state of a Tai Chi, Qigong meditative experiences.

These experiences revealed to me that I and my students had been acculturated into the idea that we had to "hang onto control," in any given situation. Control is the goal of the modern world, and it is fear based. In one of the Moving Qigong meditations we do, we simply let the body shake, letting go of all the muscles and tissue to allow the vibrations to rattle through us – loosening us, breaking up the rigidity we hold. I speak to the students as we do this about how we are taught to "keep control," and if we get "out of control" someone will often tell us to "get a grip," as if we had to walk around "gripping reality" all the time or else chaos would ensue. When we practice this Qigong exercise our goal is to absolutely let go of control, and this concept echoes through all of our Tai Chi and Qigong approach. As Lao Tzu informed us, the Tao that can be contained and controlled is not the true Tao. We have to let go of control to be lost in the flow of the Tao, and this simple effortless surrender has to be practiced, because our society and upbringing have so deeply conditioned us to hold tightly onto control.

So as we practice these Moving Qigong techniques of letting go of control over and over again, and not only does nothing bad happen, but we feel quite good, lighter, and nicer, we practice realizing what Einstein suggested, that indeed the universe IS a friendly place.

So as the Taoists showed with the Yin Yang's self-replicating image, and Chaos Mathematicians point out in their concept of self-replicating fractal reality, the microcosm contains the macrocosm. Just as our tiny individual DNA holds the image of the larger body's health, our community's health, our nation's health, and world health, my Tai Chi Meditation teacher always reminded us that our energy being was the foundation of our being; the physical was just a reflection built upon that energy world we live in, beneath the surface of what is manifest.

When we open to larger paradigms in our consciousness we become evolutionary beings, allowing a greater possibility and a greater good to flow through us. We do this by letting go of who we are, so that we can freefall, and allow the larger concepts to bloom through us in our energy Nei Gong meditations, and ultimately in our Tai Chi, as we allow our Tai Chi forms to flow through our unhinging, un-gripping body, to allow space for a larger flow to expand through us.

Both Taoists and Chaos Mathematicians see a nurturing state or balance, a positive force of equilibrium, unfolding through reality that we can learn to navigate. Chaosticians talk of attractors and strange attractors that influence the evolution of a living system – a person, or tribe, or town, company, herd, or other. Chaosticians seek to observe such systems to help them find harmony, and to be able to change. But to change in ways that evolve the system and do not tear it apart. Taoists have the same goal, but Taoists find that by looking within, we can "feel" disturbance in the field. By addressing it on an inner level we can affect the world.

My experience of absolute surrender and faith left me experiencing the entire world, and enabled my Dan Tien meditative experiences to be macrocosmic freefalls into new realities. You could say, "This boy is ca-razy!" And dismiss all I've experienced and said. And to be honest, I might have done that too, if I hadn't seen how all of this was integral to my opening to a vision of a global event. An event that lilted into my mind during meditation, and then unfolded as I surrendered everything I was, giving up my grip on all I held. So that the shipping clerk I was could be re-shaped and unfolded into the being, that would become a teacher, who would pioneer expanding mind-body practices into corporations, medical institutions, prisons, schools, and churches; to unfold and let go of my old self to become a writer, a world organizer, a media expert, a webmaster, a video producer, a medical health professional. Collecting all the medical research on the mind-body sciences of Tai Chi and Qigong for over 20 years, to spread them all across the planet to kindred spirits who collaborate on this global event each year. People who use these models for medical research, media outreach, and on and on – what we've created to educate their media and public, resulting in millions of people being affected.

My own experience of seeing how going within, that microcosm of allowing myself to "let go" and to "have faith," and to trust in a benevolent universe, allowed me to connect with human beings all over the planet in Cuba, Iran, Egypt, Israel, Russia, etc. To help them learn how to use the medical research we'd collected here in Kansas to educate their governments, to get their congresses, senates, health ministries, government offices, consulates, embassies, and the like, all over the planet to join in this effort. If I hadn't seen myself how these microcosmic ethereal lessons I had been given, or rather been willing to open to … if I hadn't seen how these microcosmic experiences of consciousness could indeed expand out and effect the external reality of our macrocosmic world … I may have dismissed their value and what they offer the world.

But, I did. So now, I hold them out to you with open hands, soft smooth pearls of wisdom I have been given. I did not sneer at them and dismiss them. I opened my heart and mind to them, and it has resulted in things that a six year old boy in Kansas could have never ever imagined in his wildest dreams.

So to recap, when doing Sitting Qigong or Nei Gong energy meditations, and thinking of an energy center or Dan Tien, just "think of it" for an instant. And then let your whole being sigh and freefall into a vastness, an all-encompassing experience. As if your whole being were floating within that energy center, or as if that energy center filled the whole universe. Have faith that everything will be okay of you absolutely let go of control, and just feel whatever lilts through you as you surrender and freefall, open to experiences larger than you can imagine, name or control. Have faith.

When doing Tai Chi, as the movements become cellular memory over time, let yourself surrender into the forms. Let the forms flow through you as you relax out of the way. Something larger and vast can flow through you as you let go. Let your being come un-hinged. Un-gripping from its old self definitions, so that an effervescent newness can expand through you with each releasing breath.

A new world, a new way, a new paradigm of existence is stretching your seams to expand through you. Tai Chi, Qigong and meditative practices are tools to allow the being, the mind, to un-grip from what it is. To allow a newness to expand through us, to become evolutionary beings.

Lao Tzu told us that we have to let go of who we are so we can become who we might be.

Taoist's Yin Yang, or Tai Chi, symbol is perhaps the original fractal art.

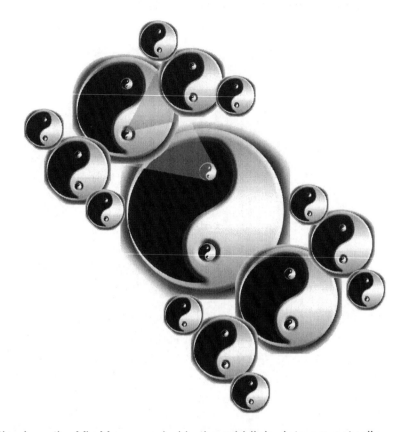

Notice how the Yin Yang symbol in the middle's dots are actually smaller Yin Yang symbols? And then notice how within them, the smaller symbols dots are actually smaller Yin Yang symbols? This was based on the Taoist concept of self-replicating reality. Of how an individuals' health determines the communities' health, and how the communities' health reflects the state's, the nation's, the world's health. Given modern science's understanding of the DNA, Taoists would say this also goes deeper. That the state of the human cell's health is determined by the health of the DNA, and the DNA by the health or balanced state of the molecules, or even atoms, of a human being. Thousands of years prior to the birth of Chaos Mathematics, Self-Replicating Theory, or computer generated Fractal Images, Taoists were sensing and beginning the study of modern Chaos Mathematics Self-Replicating Theory. Makes you think, doesn't it?

Does all this sound kind of "out there" and unrelated to real life issues? Here's how Taoist philosophy and Chaos Mathematics' validation of self-replicating theory have impacted my own work in a real tangible practical way.

I saw the Yin Yang and Chaos Mathematics self-replicating theory in practice as I began to teach Tai Chi Meditation in hospital settings (as you read in earlier chapters). I saw how profoundly it was improving the lives of medical professionals in those classes. I then saw the medical research they found in their hospital data bases were showing that scientific researchers were finding the same benefits in their study groups. The microcosm of the benefits I was seeing in my classes and have for nearly two decades was happening around the world in scientific laboratories with other people. People were able to reduce or get off of hypertension medications, or chronic pain medications, and avoid the negative side-effects of such meds, or avoid surgeries because of Tai Chi Meditation practice.

I began to research medical data showing that the modern diseases of diabetes, heart disease, and the like, that Tai Chi Meditation can help treat according to new research, are plaguing most of the planet. When we did informal calculations to see how much money our own local classes were saving our community and state in health costs, we saw the bigger Yin Yang of national and global society emerging from our smaller Yin Yang dots. We saw that literally trillions of dollars could be saved worldwide by getting Tai Chi, Qigong and mind-body meditative practices into schools worldwide.

Over the last two decades here in Kansas City, we created a macrocosm of possibility as we learned how to get Tai Chi into public schools, special education programs, drug and prison rehabilitation programs, corporate wellness (teaching in some of the world's largest corporations). We also got Tai Chi into churches and synagogues (we presented at the National Catholic Youth Conference), and into senior care (we were part of a national Tai Chi program organized by NQA co-founder, Roger Jahnke, to create a Tai Chi Efficacy Guide for Senior Care Professionals and Senior Facilities throughout the United States). Tai Chi Meditation teachers across the United States, who teach in senior care and senior activity centers, may have been partly empowered to start by Roger Jahnke and our early work.

We then incorporated how-to guides in our World Tai Chi & Qigong Day organizing and website, to help Tai Chi Meditation teachers worldwide replicate our work. We saw our work replicated in Tai Chi for Prison programs started by other Tai Chi Meditation teachers in the United States, and as far away as Australia (by Australian teacher, Bev Abella). We saw other teachers getting Tai Chi Meditation programs into churches, mosques, and synagogues. Our pioneering efforts were the microcosm. As we shared our how-to guides for free with teachers worldwide, we saw our microcosmic efforts spread out to the macrocosm of the world. Our WorldTaiChiDay.org website's page on "Tai Chi for Penal Rehabilitation" is a source link provided to penal rehabilitation professionals and institutions all across the United States, on the National Institute of Corrections website.

World Tai Chi & Qigong Day's vision is, yes, rooted in Taoist philosophy, but also is rooted in modern Chaos Mathematical theory, which validates Taoist concepts like the self-replicating microcosm of the macrocosm affect. These are not airy-fairy wanderings of the mind. These are important concepts to the future of humanity.

The Dalai Lama said that if we taught students all over the world how to meditate, violence would become a thing of the past. But this is only the beginning of what incorporating mind-body practices into the world could accomplish.

When I did a presentation at Folsom Maximum Security Prison in California, I saw how Tai Chi Meditation (Tai Chi Chih at Folsom with Judith Trethway) had reduced violence not only in the prisoners doing the mind body exercises, but also in the general population. That prison could be a microcosmic example of what Tai Chi Meditation could do for the entire planet, as these tools become part of public education worldwide.

As was stated in detail in earlier chapters, incorporating mind-body practices into public schools worldwide would not only reduce bullying and violence in the world – it would expand student's minds, enhancing their creativity, intelligence, and make them more capable of realizing the world they envision. This is scientific reality proven out by research, not pie in the sky theory.

Meditation can physically increase the empathy and compassion parts of the brain, as proven by neurological research into meditation and neuroplasticity. In 12 years we would have a whole new generation of more empathetic and compassionate humans, who were also more capable of actualizing, or actually creating, the more empathetic compassionate world their minds see and yearn for, due to the brain changes neuroplasticity research shows

Yet even more exciting, those more actualizing and more compassionate human beings all over the world would have trillions of dollars available every year, because that generation would avoid most of the common health issues facing humanity today.

Medical research shows that between 60% and 85% of illnesses sending people to the doctor can be treated or avoided by mind body practices. Again, this translates into trillions of dollars of saved health spending worldwide. The cost of incorporating mind body practices like Tai Chi and Qigong Meditation into public schools would be minimal. It would also be good for the economy, employing an army of Tai Chi and Qigong teachers worldwide who could share the treasures they have spent years practicing and understanding.

Imagine the ramifications of this! It would only cost a tiny fraction, a tiny drop, of the ocean of health cost saving these tools in education would create, to end global starvation. This more creative generation, with expanding technological revolutions, would find cheaper and cleaner ways to provide energy worldwide, adding much more annual savings, and reducing energy conflicts worldwide. This would also enabling us to save on military spending related to conflict.

Lao Tzu told us if we master our own mind, we hold the world in our hands. I was reminded of Lao Tzu's writing when I heard a story about when Bob Dylan met the Beatles. This was when the Beatles came to America at a time when their name was known by nearly every person on the planet. Dylan told the Beatles, 'You have the whole world in your hand, what will you do with it?' One of the things the Beatles did with it, was they went to India to learn meditation. That microcosmic action they took educated countless millions of people about the benefits of mind body practices, at a time long before the mountain of medical research would become available as it is today.

We know that incorporating mind body practices into public education could have profoundly positive impacts on the world, and on our global economy and ecology. The only reason it is not happening is because our individual minds have not opened to this scientifically proven reality.

When we practice our own Tai Chi, Qigong and meditative practices, we change the way we see ourselves and our world. We share this awareness with others, and institutions like healthcare, corporate wellness, government, senior care, and educational institutions. Like water dripping through a crack, this eventually opens a trickle, then a flow, then a stream, and then a flood of possibility that will wash across our planet so quickly, none of us will remember how hard it was to get that trickle started.

My wife and I have seen how hard that trickle is to get started. But we have also seen our vision of spreading this movement and mind-body technology awareness, and the science behind them. And the possibility behind them captured the imagination around the world, spurring people to pour enormous time, effort, and resources into creating more and more spectacular and larger events worldwide. It spurred people worldwide to educate their media, public, government and social institutions.

We have seen the drop that we invested our savings into nearly 20 years ago, and the 20 years of our lives, become a trickle. And it is starting to flow as global media shares this event and its vision with the world (see media worldwide: www.worldtaichiday.org/photovideogallery.html). We are not far from the dam breaking and the flood flowing.

You are the microcosm of the macrocosm of this flood. Opening our hearts and minds is how it starts. Then Yin Yang dots expand out into other Yin Yang symbols, in our communities and nations, and then out of those dots, to our world. *One World ... One Breath.*

Hong Kong's South China Morning Post Interviews World Tai Chi Day Founder

World Tai Chi Day is next Saturday, and Douglas hopes the world - and particularly the world's health organisations and professionals - will join in ...

He has staked his savings on setting up the website (www.worldtaichiday.org) and getting everything organised - the fax bill alone last month was about 15,000 dollars: what return can he possible expect?

"I don't know: I have no idea," he admitted on the phone from his home town of Kansas City. "I just know I had to try it." ...

But running classes in hospitals and prisons in the local area is one thing. World Tai Chi Day, with all the organising and cajoling and free information kits whizzing around via courier companies is quite another. How did it happen?

"Now that *is* a weird story," he said.

Douglas had originally had the idea some years ago, just after completing *The Complete Idiot's Guide to T'ai Chi & Qigong*. But after scribbling some notes to himself about how a global event could work he didn't go any further, or tell anybody about it: it seemed too ambitious, too time - demanding, too impossible to do from Kansas.

"Then a few years later, after my mother had died, my sister called me one morning and said she had this dream. She said my mother had appeared and said your brother has been writing some interesting things."

His sister had been described with an uncanny accuracy what those notes had said, and recounted how in the dream his mother had said he shouldn't have self-doubt and should follow his ideas.

It was after that phone conversation, and with the blessing of his (slightly bewildered, but supportive) wife and his two teenage children (who "did tai chi until they were teenagers when suddenly everything Dad does is wrong", Douglas said cheerfully) he "grasped the bird's tail" with both hands, and went into the project whole heartedly.

"Does your sister usually have supernatural dreams?" I asked Douglas. "No, actually she's very conservative - she was even on the election team for Bob Dole. She's not one of those flighty new age types at all." And her brother doesn't seem like that either.

His fascination with tai chi and qigong is less about the arcane spiritual side then about the physical side, and he is full of anecdotes and statistics - which he can apparently send to anyone interested by email as a database of 1,600 scientific studies - about how this is the best thing for mental and physical health since whole meal bread.

"We had a surgeon who came to the class," he said. "She'd been in a really bad car accident a few years back - and had whiplash and chronic back pain that wouldn't go away. As a doctor she had tried everything that Western science could offer and nothing helped: after two months of tai chi she went back to normal."

About 70% if illnesses, he continued, are caused by psycho-social stress: "Five million kids are on Ritalin [an anti-stress drug] - if everyone did tai chi and learned how to control stress, then half the Health system in America would be redundant."

His enthusiasm - as he talked about how tai chi and qigong are immensely sophisticated methods of cleansing the central nervous system and getting rid of past pain and trauma, as well as improving things like balance, posture and strength - was infectious.

-- The South China Morning Post, *Interview w/ World Tai Chi & Qigong Day Founder*, April 1, 2000

In Closing

I have come to see Tai Chi and Qigong as "faith walking." If you have not answered Einstein's all important question: "Is the Universe a friendly place?" with a positive yes, your Tai Chi and Qigong are not what they could be. It doesn't mean they aren't good, strong, athletic, and effective. It just means that they have not reached their highest pinnacle.

Tai Chi and Qigong are high level mind body sciences. But for many they are also powerful spiritual and personal development tools. Why? Because if you hold onto "grudges," "jealousies," "prejudice," "anger," "lust," or "hatred" in your mind and heart, it affects the way the body moves. You have to sigh, to let go, to allow a smooth flow through your body.

Biological science tells us that every thought and emotion we have is conveyed to every cell of the body via chemical processes. Of course this is just a reflection of our energy being. This all happens on a field energetic consciousness level. Then the physical body and world reflect that.

Our highest Tai Chi and Qigong movements occur when we have "let go" of as much as possible, letting go of who we are, so that we can allow what we will become to flow through us, as Lao Tzu extolled. Faith is required for us to let go. Faith that it is okay to let go.

If we, as a global society, answer Einstein's question of whether the universe is a friendly place with a "no," it will ripple out into all the decisions humanity makes. Our fear will limit our future, just like it limits the easy flow of our Tai Chi and Qigong movements. Our muscles tighten with fear when we hold fear. A new paradigm cannot unfold through us unless we have faith.

Neurological research shows that Tai Chi can increase the size of the physical brain, and research on meditation shows that it can increase the empathy/compassion part of the brain, while physically shrinking the fear/stress part of the brain. This brain change meditation can move individuals, and ultimately society, to answer Einstein's all important question with a "YES." Having less stress/fear is having more faith.

This yes answer can allow us to loosen, to surrender, to freefall into deeper states of consciousness. More vast and open states. Our physical Tai Chi and Qigong forms can provide models to practice, allowing such higher states and hopes and visions to flow through us, physically unimpeded by fear. We have to let go of the world we grip, for a new world to come.

The being who came to me said, "I am about to show you what life could be like." And then, after blowing my mind by opening my mind, and my being, and my entire universe, it reminded me, "Fear closes all doors. Fear closes all doors." New worlds open only through the faithful.

Tai Chi and Qigong can become vehicles for faith walking. It is not a religion. But for the religious person it can support a faith that your God is benevolent, and that it is okay to "let go." For an Atheist or Agnostic, Tai Chi and Qigong can help support a feeling that the "universe is a friendly benevolent place." Because they teach us that when we "let go" everything is okay.

The future of our planet depends on how we answer Einstein's question. Faith is the key.

If you enjoyed this book, you should join our free email mailing list at www.WorldTaiChiDay.org to enjoy weekly articles on breaking medical news, on Tai Chi and Qigong research, articles on Tai Chi and Taoism, and much more. **Also, you will be notified when my coming book, "The Gospel of Science," will be released.** If you liked this book you will LOVE the Gospel of Science.

The Tao of Tai Chi: The Making of a New Science is kind of a primer, or digest version, of *The Gospel of Science*, which expands on these concepts in this book, unfolding these concepts in very real tangible science based ways how those involved in spreading mind-body arts worldwide are very literally creating a new world with vast and limitless possibilities. Again, if you enjoyed this book, *The Gospel of Science* will electrify you with a hopeful anticipation of the future.

THE GOSPEL OF SCIENCE:
Where Atheism and Religion can Meet
A Quiet Revolution is Transforming Our World

By William E. Douglas, Jr.

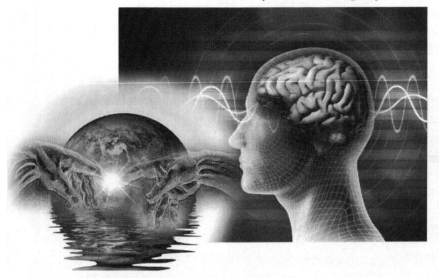

What if all it takes to change our health and our world is to simply change our minds?

A simple Kansas boy's 55 year journey into the realms of mind-body science took him around the world by taking him into the center of his own being, initially to save his own life ... where eventually his expanding journey of discovery led to a realization that science may now be leading us all to the Promised Land of milk & honey.

www.illuminationcorporation.com

If you enjoyed this book, you may also enjoy Bill Douglas's array of other widely acclaimed works ... For more information on Bill's other works, visit his websites: www.SMARTaichi.com and www.illuminationcorporation.com.

Bill's Tai Chi and Qigong book, DVD, CD:

World acclaimed instructional DVD ...
Anthology of Tai Chi & Qigong:
The Prescription for the Future by Bill Douglas
(4 hour fully instructional DVD program)

Anthology of Qigong Relaxation Therapy and Mind Expansion by Bill Douglas (CD audio of 4 tracks of Sitting Qigong, Nei Gong Energy Work Meditations)

The Complete Idiot's Guide to T'ai Chi & Qigong (4th edition, Bantam-Penguin Books) by Bill Douglas

Coming Soon, Bill's NEWEST Tai Chi Meditation DVD!

Bill's "Tai Chi Health: Powerful, Easy, Fun!" DVD will be out soon! It teaches Bill's uniquely easy and effective "Tai Chi Short Form" with Qigong Meditations—a program that has changed people's lives in his hospital programs. Combines the best of Qigong, Tai Chi, & Meditation.

[TEACHERS, if you want to learn how to teach your Tai Chi or Qigong forms in an "internal Taoist meditative health" style, this DVD can show you how. These internal teaching techniques can be adapted to any style of Tai Chi or Qigong teaching. It is about a new approach to teaching what you are teaching already, not adding new physical techniques.]

Bill has taught this Short Form with Qigong Meditation for many years, originally for people dealing with Parkinson's disease, and then later for everyone, people dealing with Heart Disease, Chronic Pain, MS, etc., and many hospital participants reported enjoying really dramatic health changes, some having their physicians take them off, or reduce their dosage, for pain medications, Type 2 diabetes meds, hypertension meds, avoiding surgery, etc.

Also, if you sign up for the free Email Mailing List at www.WorldTaiChiDay.org and select "Products" as an area of interest, you will be notified when it comes out, as WorldTaiChiDay's website announces new Tai Chi and Qigong book and other learning material releases from many masters of the Internal Arts.

Bill Douglas's Award Winning Non-Fiction:

The Amateur Parent: A Book on Life, Death, War and Peace, and Everything Else in the Universe by Bill Douglas. A series of short autobiographical events about parenthood's journey. Bill's poem from this book was "U.S. AOL-Chicken Soup for the Soul Contest" winner.

Bill Douglas's Award Winning FICTION! Bill is an award winning novelist whose unique thrillers involve cutting edge science with a Tai Chi spiritual twist ... *2012 The Awakening* by Bill Douglas (a spiritual thriller) Winner of "Best Awakening Fiction of the Year" by *Spiritual Enlightenment Magazine*

"What a gift!" -- Deepak Chopra

A Conspiracy of Spirits by Bill Douglas
(an environmental-Tai Chi-spiritual thriller)

"I highly recommend Conspiracy of Spirits! ...I read it in two days straight – eyes glued to the page! ... It's so wonderful to read a novel in which Tai Chi is an integral component. I was so moved by how it illumined other effects, ripples, from my Tai Chi practice. I can see this clearly in my own life ... Rarely have I read a novel which has taught me so much. The involvement of Tai Chi in the story, has given me a renewed reverence for my own practice ...

Several scenes were so moving, I was weeping while reading. It was very instructive, to see a character "get it," (connection) then lose it, numb out, even deny his experience, then find his way again. It was compassionate and realistic. And I can certainly relate to that. I've had extraordinary experiences from Qigong practice, but it's amazing how quickly the impact of "ah-ha's" can fade away in my mind, when covered over by the busyness and stress of having to do whatever needs done next. The next thing I know, the extraordinary experience is so far removed, that it no longer motivates me, or even seems real. It took a fiction story, to put me back in touch with what I experienced in reality!

I emerged from reading "A Conspiracy of Spirits" with a strong sense that one individual matters. Matters tremendously in this planetary crisis – the many crises we are facing together."
-- Karen Jeffers Tracy, 37 year Tai Chi practitioner

Visit author, Bill Douglas's, websites: www.SMARTaichi.com (for Tai Chi & Qigong) and www.illuminationcorporation.com (for Bill's Fiction and non-Fiction) and also visit www.WorldTaiChiDay.org to learn more about the global event Bill and his wife co-founded.

Tai Chi Therapy: The Science of Metarobics

"I have seen 3 paradigm shifts profoundly expand global use of Tai Chi and Qigong - this book will change the way Tai Chi & Qigong are approached, that modern medical science can join hands with the ancient. This seminal work should be read by every student, teacher, health professional and government health employee, and by every-one seeking a profound life and healthy society."
– Bill Douglas, Author, Speaker and Founder of World Tai Chi & Qigong Day.

"It is great to see a Tai Chi practitioner with a clinical background taking a new approach to this traditional exercise. Your work will contribute to the development of Tai Chi for people's benefit."
– Paul Lam, MD, Tai Chi for Health Institute.

Become a Healing Part of History

If you would like to get involved in a **World Tai Chi & Qigong Day** event, or to organize one of your own, learn how by visiting the official website of World Tai Chi & Qigong Day, www.WorldTaiChiDay.org or www.WorldQigongDay.org.

You will also find a plethora of free resources there, Tai Chi Medical Research on nearly 100 common health issues, video lessons and tutorials, and inspiring and moving photos and videos of WTCQD events all around the world.

You can "Join Our Free Email Mailing List" at WorldTaiChiDay.org by clicking that link, to get our free weekly email E-zine "All Things Tai Chi and Qigong" to get breaking medical and science research on Tai Chi and Qigong, and global Tai Chi and Qigong news, events, health recipes, and much more.

You can also get involved in **World Healing Day** **www.WorldHealingDay.org**. On the last Saturday of April each year, World Tai Chi & Qigong Day events have been held all over the world for nearly 2 decades. In that time events have reached out to and embraced other mind-body teachers and organizations to present and participate in their WTCQD events.

So, we decided to expand WTCQD to include these other sister mind-body practices, and other methods of opening that right-brain/creative consciousness to create an even larger worldwide wave of health and healing intent to wrap our planet in each year on World Tai Chi & Qigong Day, the "last Saturday of April."

You can get involved at:

www.WorldYogaDay.org
www.WorldReikiDay.org
www.WorldHealingMeditationDay.org
www.WorldSufiDanceDay.org
www.WorldNativeAboriginalSacredDanceDay.org
www.WorldArtDay.org
www.WorldMusicHealingDay.org
www.WorldPrayerDay.org

Learn more about author, Bill Douglas, at his personal teaching website:
www.SMARTaichi.com

Bill has produced highly acclaimed Tai Chi and Qigong DVDs, CDs, and his best-selling book is now in 4th edition. His Tai Chi and Qigong program has changed the lives of people worldwide.

Bill occasionally offers presentations around the world for major corporations, health and medical institutions, education, penal and drug rehabilitation programs, and also for Tai Chi and Qigong groups and organizations around the world. If your group is interested in hosting a presentation, you can see Bill's contact information at his website SMARTaichi.com.

A Bit About the Author ...

Without Tai Chi and Qigong I would not be walking this planet today, and none of what I've done over 40 years would ever have happened. It saved my life. I see my life as a microcosm for what these mind-body sciences can do for the entire planet.

Although you have read quite a bit about my Tai Chi and Qigong and Taoist journey, and some of my experiences as a boy that led me to that journey, there's still more to know, if you are interested in my formation, so to speak.

I received a pretty extensive religious education, because of my mother, who had been raised a Baptist, but then decided to raise me in the Lutheran Church. I attended Bible School in the summer, Sunday school all year, and got my Confirmation training. I eventually became an altar boy in the Lutheran Church.

But even as all that was happening, issues were coming to a boil. My father, who I love and respect dearly, suffered from Post-Traumatic Stress Disorders, from about three years of frontline combat. His 45th Infantry started in North Africa, then Italy, France, and finished the war in Germany. My father was in Patton's armored divisions. If you saw the Brad Pitt film, "Fury," you got a whiff of the stench my father smelled for three years. If you saw the first 10 minutes of "Saving Private Ryan," and that horrific beach landing, realize my father's 45th Infantry was involved in four beach landings. It fried him. My uncle, Dad's little brother, got out on a Section 8 (psychiatric discharge), after their very first beach landing.

My Dad was a hero to me in so many ways, as he struggled to live and work even after what he had been through. But wars come home with men, and I too suffered PTSD from his combat. It wore on me. I had a lot to untangle, and it tore us apart. I turned to drugs for some peace in my mind and life.

I became a drug addict as a teenager, and contracted Hepatitis C as a teen, and became horribly ill. The buddy who I had contracted Hep C from (when sharing dirty hypodermic needles, as I had with others many times before), eventually lost his teeth and died a couple of years later.

I however, met an angel from Hong Kong, aptly named Angela. A girl who had had a vision of Mother Mary in her garden, after her church confirmation in 1963, the same year an angel had visited me as a young boy.

I learned how to do Tai Chi and Qigong with this angel, who had done Tai Chi as a young girl with her mother. Me as a young man being driven to Tai Chi because marriage and parenthood were rearing old PTSD issues back up. Tai Chi and Qigong ended up extending my life 40 years (so far). Further than my friend who had shared the dirty needles with me and died of Hepatitis C so long ago.

In that 40 years I traveled the world and studied all I could about all spiritual and religious practices, from the Bible, to the beautifully illustrated Hari Krishna's books they handed me on the beach in California, to the *Autobiography of a Yogi* book I was given at a Hindu temple. To the Buddhist Bible, the Kabbalah, Rumi and Islamic Sufism, Native American spirituality, Aboriginal spirituality – you name it, I wanted to know about it, what it had to say.

After living through my drug addictions and finding my angel and Tai Chi and meditation, my natural curiosity of my youth came back to me. As I mentioned briefly before, when I had graduated from High School my parents came to my graduation ceremony. Of course I was high as a kite at the time (unbeknownst to my parents). However, I remember something from that night with crystal clarity. A man walked up to my parents and told them that I had been one of his most difficult Sunday school students, when I attended his classes as a young boy. When my parent's concern spread across their faces, he quickly added, "Oh, he didn't misbehave. He was very attentive, but he always had questions about the Bible that I did not have the answers to."

So apparently I had always been a seeker. And as you've seen through this book, my seeking has been without agenda. It has been a pure search for truth, no matter if it is through the cathedrals and vestibules of religion, or the clinical halls of science, my quest has been to understand, to find the truth beneath things – beyond what is understood. My nearly 60 years of travels began surrounded by the wheat fields of Western Kansas and led to the far corners of the world. Exposing me to realities science had not yet found tools to explain. And over these decades I watched science's ability expand to explain these heretofore unexplainable realities.

My conclusion is that we are all God's children (including you, Atheists, no offense intended ☺). All petals of the human flower. My personal feeling is that we are here to evolve, to bloom and become more. I feel that humanity is at a critical juncture in our human progression. That it is incumbent upon us, our generation, to learn how to change in huge ways very quickly, if we want to leave a world to our children that we would love living in.

I have come to see Tai Chi and Qigong as evolutionary tools, designed to loosen us up mentally, emotionally, and physically, so that we can not only stand the stress and strain of the demands for innovation, and change our generation must endure, but to actually be able to thrive on and enjoy the adventure this offers and entails.

No generation in the history of humanity has seen what we've seen, enduring the strain of the planet quadrupling its population in one lifetime – *ours*. No generation has both enjoyed and endured a technological revolution with the speed that we have. The stress of all this change has been and will be enormous. My own life is a template. I have lived this, a small town Kansas boy becoming a world citizen. Learning to be a webmaster, videographer, global media professional, world organizer, and evolving from a church-basement Tai Chi teacher to one commissioned by some of the largest health institutions in the world. We can evolve and change in huge ways. Without Tai Chi and Qigong I would *never* have been able to loosen and adapt as I have.

I have come to the conclusion that there is no more urgent task than to spread mind-body technologies worldwide, to as many people as fast as possible, to enable humanity to both handle and thrive during this transition we are undergoing.

As Lao Tzu said, the Tao is like water; it goes to the root of everything and nurtures all things.

This is what mind-body practices do. They dramatically improve the lives of executives and prison inmates, the poor and the rich, and they can make humanity kinder and smarter and able to create the world of our dreams, first of all by saving us trillions in avoided health costs.

These tools MUST be made part of public education worldwide. Our future's quality depends on it. Given the existing scientific research on Tai Chi, Qigong, and Meditation, it is literally insane that we have not already made them part of public education, as a hybrid of health science and physical education.

NIH research investment in Tai Chi and Qigong is incomprehensibly tiny, given the existing research on their health benefits. We know Tai Chi can increase brain size, reduce fall risks, lower high blood pressure, boost immune function, treat heart disease, and much more. Currently, very little NIH funding goes to research complementary and alternative health practices. In spite of their profound potential for preventing or treating many health issues patients face, often caused by stress. When you consider how inexpensive it would be to spread mind-body practices throughout our society via public education, healthcare, corporate wellness, senior care, and the like, it is irrational that this is not happening on a vast scale already.

Definition of insanity, Merriam-Webster Dictionary
noun in·san·i·ty
something that is very foolish or unreasonable

Definition of sane, Merriam-Webster Dictionary
adjective \'sān\
having a healthy mind : able to think normally
based on reason or good judgment : rational or sensible

The Tao of Tai Chi: The Making of a New Science Expert Reader Comment's complete text ...

I just finished this book, and I cannot say how much I enjoyed it. It is dead on with synchronicity—and a book like this has been a long time coming---the Tai Chi world has *needed a book like this* for a long time!

It takes great courage to share very personal stories of change and transformation. Bill Douglas took that step in his new book "The Tao of Tai Chi: The Making of a New Science." Bill's account of his experiences opens up doors and windows to a deeper level of meaning and Tao.

His story is expertly blended with new discoveries in science, pointing to exciting new horizons in understanding physics and experiences which currently defy explanation. From Albert Einstein to Niels Bohr, this book will take you not only on the author's own personal journey, but also to the "fingers pointing the way," of some of the greatest minds in science.

I have been waiting a long time for a book such as this. I hope it opens up the door for more teachers and practitioners of mindfulness based practices to share their own personal journey.

I suspect, based on my own experiences, and from reading those of Bill Douglas, that more people than we realize have touched levels of spirit and Tao which cannot be readily talked about. Bill opens that door to a much needed discussion, and I hope many more will follow in his footsteps. The world needs to know and understand the depths and insights to which Tai Chi and related practices can take a person.
-- Dr. Pete Gryffin, University of Florida Alumni Fellow, author of "Tai Chi Therapy: The Science of Metarobics," and founder of the Metarobic Institute.

I have practiced martial arts for more decades than most people reading this have been alive, which only really serves to say I have been exposed to many different ideas and methods of relaying Tai Chi to students of the art.

Having said that, I believe that Bill's book will excite students to keep studying deeper and learning that much of what we absorb in Tai Chi and life is Yin intuitive. I have found that any time I am breaking new ground it amazes me how many others are doing something similar—Bill's book explains how

Taoism is a way to comprehend these synchronicities, and Tai Chi helps us become subtle enough to notice them when they happen.

I was honored to review and offer my observations on Bill's latest book. Bill's latest work takes you on a journey to process the art of Tai Chi from the perspective of a westerner dealing with eastern thoughts, while showing the compensation we all make and face when attempting to adapt these philosophies and physical principles to be not just pretty sayings, but ways to live.

He does this in a typical mid westerner's "show me all the details" manner and to borrow from Bruce Lee, "Absorb what is useful, discard what is useless and add what is specifically your own". My own addition is 'retain the useless for knowledge of your opponent in battle.'

But, before getting tangled in the martial applications, the size and scope of Tai Chi is much larger than the martial applications, Bill's book tackles more than the nuts and bolts and deals with what makes it work! I always look forward to Bill's writing because he helps the people on the journey to self-reflect on the passion play in each of our lives, and shows how Tai Chi is a perfect laboratory for seeing these deeper patterns in ourselves.

-- Dave Pickens, previous National Chairman Chinese Martial Arts Division United States Amateur Athletic Union, and current National Co-Chairman of Kung Fu AAU

As Tai Chi teachers we learn about the Tao, this field of existence where all things are connected. But as a Westerner it feels too intangible and unreal. Then we experience a synchronicity that is unexplainable, and it makes one wonder if the ancient Taoists were not actually seeing a deep reality. "

When Bill asked me only 2 weeks ago to read his new book about "The Tao of Tai Chi" I felt so blessed because it was the answer to my longing to learn more about Tao. From the beginning till the end I was fascinated by the honest way Bill revealed his evolution during his journey on the way of TaiChi &Qigong. I recognized so many experiences and while reading the feeling of being part of a large Tai Chi-family became even more stronger than during our WTQD event every year.

It also brought me back to that special memory of doing the 18Taiji&Qigong in the morning on deck during my cruise in Egypt many years ago. A young man was putting the pillows on the longchairs. After a few days he said to me :"You look like an angel when you do this." ...and it was at that moment I realized that when people watch someone do Tai Chi they can feel touched by an angel, and that perhaps it was important for people to see Tai Chi. I always believed in angels so how amazed and happy I was reading just now about Bill's angelic experience at the age of six. It really confirmed it wasn't so strange to ask my Taiji angel and my students angels for help before my taijiclasses and even Lao Zhu. Some of my students know I do this, and it's OK now because,more and more people believe in angels . The insights that come during these lessons, like Bill has written, they come from the field, and give you words to explain and make difficult things easy to do. So when people say after class taiji & qigong makes them so happy, I am always overwhelmed with gratitude.

Also in 2006 our province started a project for seniors to prevent them from falling with Taiji. I was told they looked for Taiji teachers and we worked out a little initiation course. And so I began teaching in September of that year. A dream that came true.

In that year I also discovered, a global education project, called World Tai Chi & Qigong Day, which I would learn organized massive Tai Chi events in countries worldwide, and did mass publicity work to get the image of Tai Chi onto television screens worldwide and into the mind of humanity. I was immediately driven to organise it myself and so I do, every year since 2007. Every participant always feels the wonderful energy that flows around the world that day. And there are also people who just stand there, enjoy looking and I know they really are touched by the energy. This year, being the 10th time for us, it felt very special to me and although it was colder our hearts were filled with sunshine and Love. To find out, just in this year, that the founder of this wordwide project got his inspiration from an angel long long time ago, well it felt like coming home.

This book also took me back to the innocence and deepened the joy of living in Tao, in the flow in every day life because it really makes this field visible. It encouraged me to be aware even more of the tides of Yin and Yang, and to continue teaching and discovering the amazing benefits of Taiji & Qigong.

Most of all it strengthened the hope that this science of the Tao of Tai Chi, in which both the power of Yin and Yang work together in harmony, can really change our world into a better place where nobody has to live in fear or feel lonely, but can open up the heart instead, just like mine did last night. I found

back my Tao Te Ching journal and I thought: "Oh waw, the circle is round ..."
My heart was so open and wide I could embrace the whole world.

To look back and see how all of this unfolded—my experience with the deckhand saying my Tai Chi looked like an angel, and my starting WTCQD events in Europe, which the event's Founder has told me inspired other events across Europe and the world—and learning that the entire global event had been originally inspired by the Founder's angelic experience—all resulting in a a massive WTCQD happening spreading all across Europe, Asia, Oceania, North and South America, and Africa—makes one wonder if this concept of a field, the Tao that connects all minds and all things, is much more than just pretty Chinese poetry."

Thank you so much Bill for sharing all your wonderful insights and experiences and for your amazing work with WTQD. Keep on going on.

-- Hilda Cardinaels, Belgian Tai Chi teacher, and World Tai Chi & Qigong Day organizer in Belgium

The "Tao of Tai Chi" is a magical book that leads us on a Tai Chi Taoist journey into ultimate heights. Each page, each paragraph, each picture tell us that Qigong and Tai Chi, more than just a psychophysical exercise, is really a profound art, science, study and poetry that offers to us the health of body, mind and spirit. It reveals how the movements we perform in Internal Art uniting our body and our breathing can open us to infinite miracles! This book unveils just how close the *visible* and the *invisible*, the touchable and the untouchable, are! Bill Douglas reveals the simplicity in divinity and the divinity of simplicity.

-- Professor Jose Milton de Olivera, Honorary Advisor of Square of the Universal Harmony, Being Tao Association, Brasilia, Brazil

"I LOVED THIS BOOK, really lovely! This book took me into a very deep trip internally and what I liked the most was that Bill was able to connect Art with philosophy, science, and more specifically with consciousness science in a way that seemed very easy and simple, as simply elegant as a flower opening. It is an awakening tool for everyone to realize how strong is our inner and how it feels easy and simple when we are connected to our true self. It highlights how important that balancing the self and reaching harmony is the way of well-being and a better life. As the Tao of Tai Chi: The Making of New Science show, this author's "following the Tao" has literally changed the world. I would like first to Thank Bill Douglas for his efforts to spread the idea of World Tai Chi & Qigong Day, and I would like to thank everyone worldwide who carried and shared this idea around the planet. And I would like to thank everyone in Egypt who helped in Egypt's World Tai Chi & Qigong Day; Actually, Egypt's WTCQD is the result of sharing love and compassion. It started as a very small idea till it reached all Egypt through the national TV and newspapers and also the International media coverage especially after all the changes that Egypt passed through lately. So WTCQD turned to be for Egyptians and also the world more than just an event but it turned to be a call for Peace and a representation of how we can pass through the Consciousness's storms around the planet these days. Actually, I was trying to organize the event to be like that, helping the people to raise their awareness and their vibrations about the importance of being connected internally and find the true self. I remember the first event in Egypt of WTCD was a small number of people and I was leading them as the Tai Chi and Chi Kung Expert for 2 hours, our last event was the 8th one and it lasted for 12 hours of continuous activities and lectures covering as much as we can on the mind, body science with more than 15 instructors from different nationalities; Egyptians, Indians, Chinese, Lebanese, English, Americans, Dutch all of them are living in Egypt. We also had more than 5000 people all over the day attending the event. The event is more than just an event for everyone, it is a day to be connected to our self, reach balance and harmony, get a small touch from heaven to know and understand the real taste of being free from the inner prison reaching the inner freedom. Actually, the real freedom is deeply inside our self, not to be found by seeking it outside and I remember the saying of Ali ibn Abi Talib "You may Presume you are a small entity, But within you is enfolded the entire universe. Your Remedy is within you, but you do not sense it. Your Sickness is from you, but you do not perceive it." When we recognize that we have the most powerful tool and with that, we can change our life and bring all the good we wish to our self. we realize then that the profound tool is simply our heart. The power of Heart is the power of Love. The Tao of Tai Chi: The Making of a New Science explains in Practical usable way to understand that this insight brings all the prophets and philosophers and all the human kind good work together, in order to recognize that the universe and our great solutions to our great challenges, lie within us. And this power of love is reflected throughout the pages of this modern readable version of ancient wisdom.

-- Mohamed Essa, Chromatic Healing Founder, Official World Healing Day Organizer, World Tai Chi & Qigong Day Organizer, Cairo, Egypt

If you enjoyed this book, you will love the author's other books, DVDs, and CD exploring the Tao of Tai Chi and life ...

BOOKS:

"The Gospel of Science"

"The Complete Idiot's Guide to T'ai Chi & Qigong" (4th edition)

World acclaimed instructional DVD ...
Anthology of Tai Chi & Qigong: The Prescription for the Future by Bill Douglas (4 hour fully instructional DVD program)

Anthology of Qigong Relaxation Therapy and Mind Expansion by Bill Douglas (CD audio of 4 tracks of Sitting Qigong, Nei Gong Energy Work Meditations

Award Winning Tai Chi Spiritual Thriller Novel's by the "Tao of Tai Chi" author ...

"A Conspiracy of Spirits"   "2012 The Awakening"

Reader comments:
"What a gift!" – Deepak Chopra

"Best Awakening Fiction of the year!"
-- Spiritual Enlightenment Magazine

"I highly recommend Conspiracy of Spirits! ... it's so wonderful to read a novel in which Tai Chi is an integral component. I was so moved by how it illumined other effects, ripples, from my Tai Chi practice. I can see this clearly in my own life ... Rarely have I read a novel which has taught me so much. The involvement of Tai Chi in the story, has given me a renewed reverence for my own practice ..."
-- Karen Jeffers Tracy, 37 year Tai Chi practitioner

Award Winning non-Fiction by "Tao of Tai Chi" author ...
"The Amateur Parent: A Book on Life, Death, War & Peace, and Everything Else in the Universe"

Learn more about the author of "The Tao of Tai Chi: The Making of a New Science," and his other books, DVD, CDs, at:
SMARTaichi.com   illuminationcorporation.com

Made in the USA
Lexington, KY
16 September 2016